Library Displays

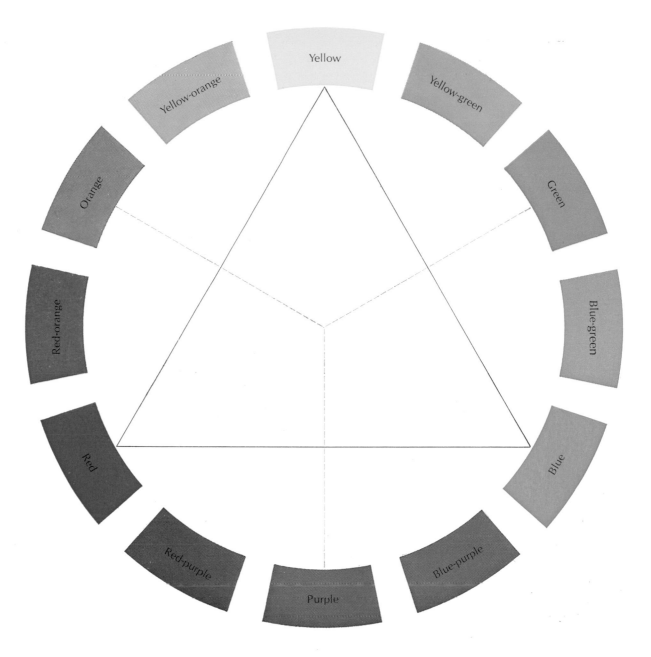

Library Displays

Their purpose, construction and use

by Mona Garvey

The H.W. Wilson Company • New York 1969

To my family and to L. B.'s family

Acknowledgments

The author wishes to thank the many people who read drafts of the manuscript and offered criticism and advice: Reba Anderson, Jan Cle-vellan-Broune, Milton Byam, Leontine Carroll, Mrs. Persis Donahue, Mrs. Clara Garvey, Dr. James Lieberman, Mrs. Lucille Lieberman, Dr. Annette Hoage Phinazee, and Mrs. Susan Murtha Ryan.

Special thanks are due to the School of Library Service of Atlanta University, where most of the research for the book was completed, and to the DeKalb Branch of the Brooklyn Public Library where many of the display ideas were tested.

Contents

1. Introduction

Bulletin boards and displays can be the nemesis of many librarians. Most of us hold at least minimum credence in the theory that libraries should devote space to displays of some kind. Many of us are hazy as to exactly why this should be done, but the fact that display areas are usually provided indicates that one is expected to make use of them. An additional complication is the prevailing belief that displays require artistic ability and a certain knack which one either has or does not have. This belief has probably been perpetuated because it is comforting to our artistic inadequacies, but it is false. Artistic ability is undoubtedly useful, but it is not at all essential to the preparation of effective displays. What is essential in the absence of such talent is the development of a new attitude toward displays based on a few principles and learnable skills.

Unfortunately our education has provided many of us with neither the proper attitude nor the principles and skills for the job. Few if any colleges or universities offer general courses in display work, and most library courses do little more than refer to the subject in passing. Art and display work on the part of amateurs seem to fall into that category of things which one is simply to do, or not to do, as best one can. Too often our unskilled and unprepared best is insufficient to the task.

Many of us are unaware of our lack of preparation until we are suddenly confronted with empty bulletin boards which we are expected to fill, cover, or hide. We may discover that we have no ideas regarding what to place on the boards or how the material should be arranged. We often resort to simply covering the space with whatever material we can obtain quickly. The space is often covered with public service bulletins, posters advertising community or cultural events, or miscellaneous book jackets. These tactics do cover the space in one way or another, but, unless there is a definite plan, any similarity between merely covering the space and using it constructively is accidental.

If we wish to *use* the space rather than simply cover it, there are a number of ways in which we can seek help. Our first impulse is probably to ask one of our more experienced fellow workers what he or she does about the problem of bulletin boards. We may find that experience in the field has not solved that particular problem. We may be given ideas about useful sources of display material, but there is a good chance that we will not find adequate information on arranging it. Since we know or suspect the limitations of our "best" in this area, we may continue our search.

Professional journals are directed toward on-the-job employees dealing with on-the-job problems and are often a good source of ideas. A few of the journals offer display suggestions on a more or less regular basis, in which case they usually rely on material sent in by others in the field. Most of the material is on the order of "What We Did for Columbus Day" or "Our Exhibit for Thanksgiving." The artistic level of the displays is often less than noteworthy, but the interest, enthusiasm, and ingenuity in use of materials is frequently an incentive to others doing displays. The special validity of these "by and for amateurs" displays lies in the fact that most of them have been created and executed by others of limited artistic ability, that the materials required are usually easily available and inexpensive, and that the ideas are simple and easily duplicated or adapted. The chief drawback in imitating these displays is the fact that some of the ideas are trite and poorly executed, and that these ideas are often published and copied right along with the good ones.

A few of the professional journals offer a once or twice a year coverage of the whole publicity program, and, in this case, the articles are usually written by professional artists or public relations specialists. Many of the articles are excellent, but they are often by, about, and for other professionals and specialists. Some of the specific suggestions may be of use, but many of the suggestions cannot be simplified to fit either limited skills or low budgets. We can only wish that we were as competent as the authors of the articles, or that we could hire their services for our own library.

Some of the educational and recreational supply companies attempt to bridge the skills gap by making various types of display kits. Some of these kits are assemble-it-yourself display backgrounds—which means that one has an attractive background, but it is still up to the individual to choose and arrange the display materials. Such kits can be very useful, but they should not be purchased unless you have a clear idea of how you want to use them. This kind of display background will not solve all display problems; it may *help* to solve them, but it will do so only to the extent that time and effort have been devoted to the effective use of it.

There are complete kits for displays which are especially designed for libraries and educational institutions. All one need do is put them up. Their chief drawback, other than the sometimes high price tag, is that they are of necessity general in approach and cannot be personalized to fit specific needs. They are useful to have on hand when a professional display is needed for a special occasion, but obviously they cannot meet the day-to-day display needs of most libraries.

There are, of course, many books and pamphlets which purport to tell "all" about displays and how to do them. These range from compendiums of standard ideas for all standard occasions, to manuals which practically guarantee to make you an expert at lettering in ten easy, fifteen-minute lessons. The level of artistic ability called for ranges from duplicating patterns (trace, fold, and cut) to following a step-by-step breakdown of a display done by a professional artist. The former approach is frequently insulting to our intelligence, if not to our limited ability, and many of the cutouts are not worth tracing, folding, and cutting. The latter technique is evidently offered on the assumption that professionalism can be achieved by anyone if presented in small enough steps; this is flattering but not too realistic.

There are also many middle-ground books and pamphlets which assume the presence of some limited abilities and further assume that these can be improved upon with effort. Some of these books concentrate on various aspects of display work, construction advice for assembling various types of boards and displays, lettering, specific display ideas, design principles, and so forth. All of these materials are useful; some are very well done and very practical, and even the poorer ones have some usable ideas to offer. There are other books which attempt to cover the whole field of display work. This book is of the latter type, but it differs in one important respect.

Most of the general display books attempt to present display ideas which will be useful to librarians, teachers, and recreation specialists. These three professions share many similar display problems, but there are many differences. Each profession is dedicated to a different purpose, requires different education and training, serves a different clientele, and operates within a different framework and environment—and each profession requires a different type of display program. The general ideas presented in this book are applicable to displays in almost any field, but the approach and the specific display ideas are geared to the unique problems of libraries and librarians. Emphasis is placed on why displays should be done and how they should convey ideas; there are discussions on function and types of displays, on sources of display ideas, on design elements and principles and how they work in practice. There are also short-cut ideas for adaptable design backgrounds, multipurpose cartoons and captions, and some fast, easy types of lettering. Each of these discussions includes specific examples for library displays and offers suggestions to help librarians to create original displays.

There is one important thing to keep in mind when reading this book or any other in this field: no one book, pamphlet, or article will solve all display problems. The skills which you have, the skills which you lack, and the situation in which you are working are all unique; there can be no general source or approach which will meet your exact specifications. Therefore you have to collect the bits and pieces which will add to your skills, smooth over your non-skills, and help you to do your job more easily and effectively. You will have to read as many books, pamphlets, and articles as possible; keep on the alert for adaptable ideas in other libraries, classrooms, and in department stores, groceries, advertisements, etc. It is a never-ending job to collect display ideas and to use them well; but if one has to do displays or supervise their execution, it is a professional responsibility to do the job well. It is hoped that this book will help you to do it better.

2. Patron X and the library

Let us assume that Patron X is entering the library for the first time. We will further assume that Patron X is an average library user, or non-user, who is rather limited in his knowledge of the library and its services, and that he has entered a typical library (if there is such a thing). Patron X may or may not be seeking something particular in the way of materials or services; he may simply be checking out the situation for future reference, or killing time during his lunch hour or while waiting for an appointment.

He enters the library. What does he see? What he probably sees is the circulation desk and some rather busy-looking people, one of whom may be sitting behind a sign indicating that he or she dispenses information. There may also be a few basic informational signs relevant to due dates, fines, or the sale of shopping bags. There is a general bustle of activity, and the people approaching the desk all seem to be familiar with the procedure.

In a larger library there may be a guard on duty or someone at the door to check outgoing books. Patron X may not have encountered this before: is the guard or checker there to check library cards? If Patron X loiters in the lobby, will the guard suspect him? Should he ask permission to use the library, or should he hurry through the lobby as though he knew where he was going? The desk procedures, the "Someone" on duty at the information desk, and the possible presence of a guard or book checker are just a few of the things which may disturb Patron X when he enters the library.

Since no one likes to step into an unfamiliar situation, and since each library is different in arrangement, operation, and service, the whole first impression might make Patron X feel embarrassed and ill at ease. He may be reluctant to admit his uneasiness or the fact that he has not been in a library since school days; and therefore he may be hesitant about asking for help even if someone at the information desk looks receptive and not too busy. Besides not knowing exactly what the library has to offer, Patron X may have an additional problem in not really knowing what help he needs. What he really requires on this first visit is general orientation whether or not he seeks specific information; in fact, if Someone should approach him and offer assistance, he might claim to know what he is looking for and beat a hasty retreat.

Assume that Patron X bypasses the main desk and decides to go it alone. He has, of course, no idea of the arrangement of the library, so he may find himself in a cul-de-sac in the children's or the young teen room. Since immediate retreat would call attention to his error and make him look foolish (or so he thinks) he may have to feign interest in some of the books. Here, too, he might be embarrassed if another Someone offers to help him. If Patron X is intrepid enough to continue his self-conducted tour, the same situation may repeat itself in each section of the library.

All the poor soul wants is to be inconspicuous, look around, and get some idea of what the library has to offer. This is extremely difficult to do when it seems to him as though the other patrons know exactly what they are looking for and how to find it. He may be further confused by differences between this library and others: he may wonder whether this library has current magazines and newspapers, or whether only some libraries offer this service; he may be confused by the subject divisions since, in his school library, all the books were kept together; he may wonder why the stacks are closed (or open) here —there may be literally hundreds of differences between this library and any other Patron X may have used.

There are all kinds of information Patron X might like to have, but it may be difficult for him to ask and expose his ignorance. This may

sound a trifle extreme, but so many things today are self-service that many of us find it difficult to ask for information, especially in the area of free service; we may be hindered by our own ignorance of the procedure or simply reluctant to "bother" anyone with our vague questions. For whatever reason, we may decide to do without information rather than risk being rebuffed or made to feel inadequate or stupid.

Now then, let us add some displays to make information a little more accessible and send Patron X back to the entrance. What does he see when he enters this time? The same scene as before plus a few displays and directional aids. There is perhaps a lobby display of photographs (or prints, old maps, documents, books—anything of educational, cultural, or community interest); there is a display calling attention to special library programs or services; and there is a large floor plan of the building.

At the very least these displays give Patron X an excuse to loiter and something to look at while he surveys the situation. Is the guard or someone else watching him? Does that person look grouchy or helpful? Are others asking for information at the desk? The display on programs or materials may stimulate Patron X's interest in a particular item or service; and it will at least provide him with some indication of what is available to him in the library—he may never have heard about the noon-hour lectures, the print collection, the phonograph records, the educational films, or the large-print books.

The floor plan may furnish Patron X with sufficient information to locate what, if anything, he wants; and it will give him an idea of the arrangement of the building and provide clues to the types of materials to be found in the various sections. If he wishes to browse through the library, the plan will help him to locate those areas in which he might be most interested and to avoid those in which he has no interest. Furthermore, and perhaps most important, the mere presence of the displays and the floor plan establish the fact that there are others who do not know their way around and who are not necessarily expected to know.

In addition to these services, the displays give Patron X a frame of reference if he does wish to ask for specific information. He is now able to ask whether the photography books are in the nonfiction or the reference section (even though he may be in doubt about what the nonfiction and reference sections are exactly); he can ask whether sports magazines and daily papers are in the reading room (since the floor plan has told him that there is such a room); and he may ask how one checks out the records, paintings, and large-print books which are mentioned in the display, or whether one needs a library card to attend the noon-hour lectures or films.

To the person at the desk the questions may sound as uninformed as they would have without the displays, but they undoubtedly sound better to Patron X. Without the displays, he may not have had the courage to ask what he needed to know. He has been provided with some questions for openers, and if Someone is helpful he may then make further inquiries about services and procedures. What the aids have given him, in effect, are a few psychological props to help him get oriented in a new situation. Supplying these props is simply good manners on the part of the library.

Patron X continues his tour of the library, though this time around he has some idea of where he is going and what kinds of materials he can expect to find. Each department has a floor plan and/or directional signs indicating where certain materials are located. If there is anything at all unusual in the arrangement (if, for instance, oversize books or paperbacks are in a separate section) there is a sign directing attention to that fact. If mysteries, science fiction, or new books are in a special section, or if they are interfiled but marked with colored tapes, that is indicated.

There is a sign or poster telling the patron what the vertical file contains, and whether or not he may use the file freely or should ask permission. There is a sign posted near the current magazines which indicates the location of *Readers' Guide* and tells where the bound magazines are kept; there is a sign near the newspapers indicating whether or not back copies may be consulted. If there are copying or reading machines the directions for use are clearly given, and there is an added note reminding the patron to ask the librarian for help if it is needed. If there is a separate reference department, it has a floor plan which includes a list of the ten most-used sources with the location of each indicated on the plan; if some books are kept at the desk, that fact is mentioned; and there may be a display explaining the use and arrangement of one particular type of reference source. There is, in short, a general air of helpfulness throughout the library which reflects an obvious desire to inform and serve the patron. In each section there are ice-breaker displays directing attention to arrangement, materials, and services of which the patron may have been unaware. There is ample opportunity for Patron X to inform himself by browsing, and an environment for asking questions is provided.

We have seen what displays can do for Patron X, but let us not forget that Someone at the main desk and in each of the departments stands to gain too. While Patron X is looking over the floor plan, the librarian can be looking over Patron X. Does he appear to be a first-time user? is he looking at the list of reference books? does he appear to need help? If the librarian decides that help is indicated, he or she can refer to the floor plan in offering it. Instead of a direct and possibly intimidating "Are you looking for something?" an indirect "May I show you where something is on the plan?" may be used. The

patron and the librarian can discuss the floor plan rather than Patron X's lack of knowledge, and the librarian can use the floor plan to take Patron X on a stationary tour of the library or the department. The location of materials can be pointed out on the plan; this is more satisfactory than pointing "over there" and it provides personal service without the necessity of leading the patron to the spot—it can be particularly useful in libraries where some materials are kept on a balcony.

These examples apply to a fairly large library, but the same principles are operative even in a one-room facility. There are always materials in drawers, files, and backrooms of which the casual browser is unaware; and he feels too intimidated for undirected browsing (under the seemingly suspicious eye of the librarian), especially in a small library. When only one librarian is available there is a greater chance that he or she will be occupied and unable to provide information when the patron needs it. Therefore, even in a small library, the various kinds of displays can be of assistance to both patron and librarian; there can be some "come-in" posters or displays, some directional aids (and remember that even when all materials are in view, the arrangement is *not* obvious to the patron). Especially in a school library, there should also be some self-help displays on reference sources.

In large and small libraries, public, school, and university libraries, the displays can assist in de termining where and when assistance should be provided and enable the staff to provide it more effectively. The various displays will be useful in formal or informal classes and tours; they can be displayed in various public places to promote library usage, services, and support; they can be employed to explain the library's function to your supervisory authority—principal, superintendent, dean, school board, board of trustees—or to the real source of support and the reason for your services—your public.

A service function is always difficult to "sell," explain, and evaluate; and displays of various types can be of assistance in selling the tax-paying public and the budget makers on the value and function of the library and of the various departments in it. People do not use, buy, or support what they do not see, and publicity can help them to see the library.

3. The publicity message

Now that it has been indicated, in a general way, what publicity can do for the patron and for the librarian, more specific ideas about publicity may be given. There are scores of publicity techniques, but the chief concern here is with visual publicity. This type of publicity may be divided into internal and external varieties; that is, publicity employed outside the library (the come-on) and that employed inside the library (the come-in). Publicity for the various departments may be similarly subdivided: publicity used within the department itself and that used elsewhere in the library to publicize the particular department.

Publicity may also be divided according to the type of message it is intended to convey and according to the visual form of the message. The type of message and the type of form are interrelated in that the message can dictate the form, and, if the form is selected first, it can influence the manner in which the message is presented. The same message can be conveyed in a number of different forms, but each form will deliver it in a different way and with a different emphasis. The message itself—the what, why, and how of it—is of greater importance, so that aspect of publicity will be dealt with first.

Whatever the message or form, all publicity for the library should attract attention; if you do not attract attention, no one will get the message you have to deliver. All publicity should, of course, have a message. One type of message might be called institutional image making. It should call attention to educational, cultural, historical, or community matters—with the implication that the library has been and still is an important factor in their development.

Institutional image making

A display projecting an institutional image is a prestige production offered in the public interest. A display of library materials may be included if they are directly relevant to the subject, but no direct "selling" of the library should be done. If related library materials are available, they could be displayed nearby, but the connection between the two displays should be as subtle as possible. The possibilities for this type of display are almost limitless: displays of original art work or reproductions; historical documents significant in national or local history; manuscripts; photographs important for artistic merit or historical or educational significance; educational displays on community matters—voting procedures, civic organizations, community government, displays dealing with the school system; a series of displays based on significant observations made by world leaders or figures important in American history; old maps; and other items of historical, artistic, or educational interest. These materials may be available in your library, or they may be borrowed from other libraries, museums, newspapers, industries, publishers, civic groups, or the general public.

Arranging and setting up this type of display requires a great deal of thought, time, and effort —and it will probably disrupt library operation somewhat—but it is worth it. This kind of display can attract people to the library who would otherwise not have come, and it can do much toward establishing contacts with other public institutions and civic groups in the area. These displays can be most effective in calling attention to the library as an important public institution, and as an active, contributing part of the community rather than the monolithic, stagnant institution which the public often considers it to be.

Personal image making

A second type of image making is of a more personal kind; it is intended to foster a personal relationship between the library and the patron. It should establish the fact that the library is on the side of the patron, and in return, should help put the patron on the side of the library. This type of display should explain something about the organization and function of the library; where the money comes from and how it is spent; what recent problems and successes the library has had; how the library was founded; how the library has figured in community affairs; what the personnel of the library actually do (in addition to the routine tasks the public may see); what training or education is required for the various positions in the library; how the various departments function; what services the library provides and why (and what services they do not provide and why not); library policies regarding book selection; and the what and why of library operation—such things as fines, overdue notices, closed stacks, checking of books at the exit, hours of operation, and so forth.

That is a rather lengthy list of facts about the library, and it may appear to be too much to convey through posters and displays. But remember, please, that publicity is a continuous operation which cannot be relegated to one week a year or even one day a month. If a continuing plan is adopted to inform patrons of new policies and services, changes, and standard operations, all of these things will, in time, be covered. What should be recognized is the fact that the patron as a library user and as a taxpayer has a right to all of this information, and that the library has an obligation to provide it. It should, however, be offered in such a way that it will be of interest and use to the patron as well as of benefit to the library and the staff.

The problem is how to present this type of publicity effectively. A dull display saying, "Library Services Are ..." or "Library Policies Are ..." or "The Library Budget Is ..." is not the way. Try to be as interesting and varied as possible in your presentation. It is not, unfortunately, intrinsically fascinating information, so it should be made as palatable as possible. One of the best approaches is to be rather off-hand about it or to use soft-sell humor. Possible captions are: "Just Thought You Might Be Interested ...," "Would You Believe ...?," "We Just Wanted to Tell You ...," "Have You Heard About ...?," "Bet You Didn't Know ...," and "May We Remind You ...."

To be more specific: suppose some of the patrons are annoyed by the library's policy of checking books at the door; a bulletin board or poster might be put up saying, "We Know That YOU Don't Steal, but ...." The poster might then add a bit of information about materials being taken, apologize for possible inconvenience to the patron, and ask forbearance. This technique might also be used to explain why the library collects fine money and how the money is spent; the caption "We Don't Want to Rob You, but ..." might serve as an introduction to the information—and a cartoon of a man with his hands up would add to the message. A soft-sell, humorous approach may be used to explain any library policies which patrons often do not understand.

The trick is to present the policy in such a way as to put the patron on the side of the library; the information is offered as something which *might* be misunderstood, so it is being explained "just in case" and because the patron has a right to know.

A policy of offering and sharing information should, over a period of time, make the patrons better informed about libraries in general and your library in particular. Patrons should feel that they are members of, rather than just users of, the library—that the library has a personal interest in them and their needs and that they should take an active interest in the library. A long-term program of informing the public about library operation and costs and the training and responsibilities of librarians and other staff members should develop greater awareness of what the library is all about. When budget time comes around, there should be more community understanding of why library operation costs what it does and why salaries are what they are (or why they should be more). The public needs to know these things and you, as a librarian, need to have them known. That aim cannot be accomplished in a day, a week, or a month.

Directional messages

Another type of display, of more direct and immediate benefit to the librarian and to the patron is the directional variety; its chief function is to help the patron locate something.

Included in this group would be floor plans, signs and displays to assist in the use of the card catalog (and if there are other catalogs in the library that fact should definitely be mentioned), signs near the catalog indicating the location of reference or oversize books (or any other materials kept where patrons might have difficulty in finding them), signs on book cases indicating the range of numbers or letters and the subject category, and signs on vertical file cabinets indicating the contents.

There could also be cross references from one section to another; a sign in the 960 section could refer the patron to 916 for descriptive information about Africa, or suggest that the patron consult the vertical file for supplementary information; a sign in the biography section could mention that collective biographies are in the 920's—it might also be suggested that the patron consult biographical sources ("ask the librarian") for information about a person; if there is another biographical section in the library (in the children's or young teen room) that too should be indicated. All of the information conveyed by this type of sign is basic, so basic in fact that many librarians mistakenly believe that it is not necessary to call attention to it.

Such an attitude may be flattering to some patrons, but it makes it difficult for the less well-informed person to admit his deficiencies and ask for assistance. Let us admit that most patrons are uninformed about the variety of materials and services offered by the library. It is better practice to risk insulting through an excess of information than risk overlooking the needs of the poorly oriented library user, and that advice applies to adults and children. Once again, this type of assistance is simply a matter of good manners in relating to users of the library.

Training aids

Still another type of message, even more overlooked than a sufficient variety of directional signs, is what might be called a training aid or self-help display. It is more than a sign and less than the usual display; its purpose is to inform and assist the patron in regard to library sources; it falls in line with the theme of interpreting the materials to the user, a theme so often mentioned in library literature. This aid should direct attention to a particular book or type of book of which the patron may be unaware. A patron cannot ask for information or an information source when he does not know of its existence.

This display could refer to a source (index, bibliography, thesaurus, handbook, or whatever) and give some indication of the type of information it contains and the uses to which it can be put. The book itself, or a facsimile of one of the pages, could be used with an explanation of the entries and mention of similar sources. To be most effective, particularly in a school or college library, this display should be changed once a month and the display for the previous month placed elsewhere in the library or school—thus becoming a "come-on" for the library or a department of the library rather than a "come-in."

Another kind of display in this category is an information display based on material available in reference sources. It is somewhat more general than the training aid and calls attention to types of information available in the library rather than specific sources. This display might be based on charts of interest rates for loans, voting procedures, baseball statistics, facts about famous people, travel information—anything that might be of interest to your particular clientele. The intent is to give an indication of the wide variety of information obtainable in library materials.

"Teasers"

Yet another category is a kind of floating display which might be termed a "teaser." These displays are not intended to provide specific information or to call attention to specific sources or kinds of sources, but to call attention to general aspects of library service and operation (some would be of the image making variety). Most would be quizzes of one kind or another or "Did You Know?" displays. A quiz might be a list of questions which could be answered from one of three listed books—which one? It could be a list of terms—*bibliography, index, almanac, yearbook*—to be matched with a list of definitions. It could be a true-or-false quiz about library

operation or library policies. It could, in effect, be anything to test knowledge or pique curiosity and to call attention to various library departments or services.

This kind of teaser display is quite versatile and it can be used to disseminate information, or to dissipate misinformation, about library operation. For instance, there could be a multiple-choice quiz on the cost of various library materials and processes: The average cost of a book is ...; The average cost for processing a book is ...; The cost of binding a book is ...; The average book requires ... catalog cards. This kind of quiz could be used to compare library services in the United States with those in other countries: The United States has ... public libraries and ... school libraries; Russia (or England, France, etc.) has ... public libraries (or volumes, research libraries, librarians, etc.). It can also be used to tell the patron about the number of books, periodicals, records, pamphlets, films, filmstrips, or reproductions the library has available—and how these holdings compare with those of other libraries of the same size. The quiz technique is entertaining and effective, and it is an effective way of getting all kinds of useful information across to the patron.

Since a teaser display is aimed at the browser, attractiveness and simplicity are the chief ingredients (after the idea, of course); there should be a drawing and/or caption to attract attention; the layout should be as simple as possible; and the answers should be on the same board (possibly under a lift panel) or posted nearby. The caption, cartoon, and questions should all be slanted toward the expected viewers; adults, teenagers and children will all be attracted by different types of questions. It should also be kept in mind that this is a very good type of display to send out to meetings of persons interested in the library and to various public places.

Book-pushing messages

And still another kind of display, and the kind used by all libraries, is of the book-pushing variety. The simplest approach is simply to push newly arrived books or best sellers, but there are many other techniques which could and should be used. An effort should be made to come up with unusual groupings of books and with spin-off selections based on current events. During election years one can capitalize on the possible interests of the various candidates; groupings can be made under "Books (Names) Should Read" and included could be books on public speaking, politics, government, law enforcement, and history, as well as biographies of politicians. When prominent people receive government appointments the same technique could be used. A new ambassador to France might be offered books on French history, French grammar, travel in France, the Common Market, French cooking, and French art, music, and literature. The same approach could be taken with

historical figures; perhaps Columbus should have read books on navigation, map making, foreign travel, American Indians, and travel in the United States. The possibilities are unlimited; members of the staff are a good source of suggestions on people and the books they should read or should have read.

Department store techniques could be adapted in the form of "specials" on books; there could be a jumble table of older books which may be checked out for double the usual time, or a display of paperbacks still in the shipping carton (to which they have been returned after processing). Unfinished shelves might be borrowed from a store and used to display books on wood finishing; books on gardening might be displayed in a wheelbarrow. Use any device or grouping which may interest, amuse, or intrigue your patrons.

Holidays and special events

A final type of display is that devoted to holidays or special events. It has been mentioned last because it is usually a bore; there is nothing more dreary than an obligation board which looks like one. The reason that it is usually a bore is a very simple one: the message has been lost or forgotten. With no message mere decoration is left; and the decoration, all too often, is a collection of the standard and probably trite ideas appropriate (or inappropriate) to the event. If a holiday cannot be ignored (and some of the lesser ones such as Valentine's Day may be ignored or noted with a "Yes, it is Valentine's Day, isn't it?") then an attempt should be made to be original, informative, amusing, or at least as simple as possible.

One way of handling a special event is to make a quiz of it: "How Much Do You Really Know About George Washington?" (or Lincoln, Columbus, Christmas, Hanukkah, Valentine's Day, Groundhog Day, Memorial Day). Questions about people should include the standard dates and what they did and also mention a few personal items such as whether or not Washington had children and when Lincoln grew his beard; and the answers should include the sources of the information. Questions about religious holidays could refer to the history and forms of observance; questions about special days could ask when they were first observed and why. Depending on the information available, and how well known the subject is, the quiz could be either true-or-false or multiple-choice.

The opening section of chapter 6 offers some suggestions on effective display backgrounds; many of these backgrounds need only a simple addition to make a completed board. A collection of short quotations of a religious, educational, cultural, or historical nature could be available when a special occasion board is needed; quotations could be printed in advance and used against one of the suggested backgrounds. If the board is well designed and the quotation appropriate, display purposes will be served.

These, then, are the kinds of messages which the library should be propagating. In summary: institutional image making of a general or personal kind; directional messages; training aids on types of sources and displays indicating kinds of information available; teaser displays for miscellaneous information about the library; the "read books" message; and the holiday and special events message. It was mentioned previously that each of the messages can be offered in various forms and that the various forms will present the messages in different ways; some forms are more suitable for certain messages, but often the same message can be presented equally as effectively through a variety of forms.

4. Forms of visual publicity

In theory there are four different forms of visual publicity which serve different functions and require different approaches. The terms are overlapping and are used interchangeably so that it is sometimes difficult to determine where one stops and another starts. The four forms of visual publicity are signs, posters, bulletin boards, and displays.

Signs

A sign is a lettered notice which is intended to advertise something or to give directions or a warning, and it is probably one of the most abused and misused members of the publicity family. Signs have all too often been relegated to telling people not to do things, and, with the possible exception of supermarket and department store signs, they often do not tell us where we are supposed to go or what we are supposed to do in an unfamiliar situation. In the library, or in any public institution for that matter, no prior knowledge should be assumed. Patrons should be told everything from the fact that library cards are free to whether or not there are restrooms. They should be told to "Return Books Here" and "Check out Books Here" (the presence of a photographic check-out machine is not sufficient to indicate to the patron the place where books are checked out). Patrons should be told where they may go in the library and where they may not go (if there is a separate section or a second floor, a patron may not be sure whether it is part of the public area of the library or a work area). If there are vertical file cabinets, it should be indicated whether or not the patron has free access to them. All of this information may seem obvious to the librarian, but it is not necessarily obvious to the patron. It is true, of course, that many signs will go unheeded by many people, but the signs should be there for those who need them and who will notice them.

Signs should not be cryptic notices taped here and there throughout the library. They should be fresh and clean and should be replaced at the first sign of old age. If there are a number of signs in the same general area, they should be the same size (unless the messages vary too much in length), and they should be on the same color poster board and printed in the same type and size of lettering. Preferably each sign should be map tacked to a larger piece of painted or burlap covered homosote or bristle board (both are types of fiberboard sold in sheets). If the signs cannot be propped on a flat surface or nailed in place, they can be taped in place with rolled strips of masking tape (sticky side out) or with double-faced tape placed on the back of the sign or support. They should not be affixed with transparent tape since that looks hasty and sloppy and it turns brown and old looking rather quickly. Signs of special importance and interest can be made more attractive and effective by means of a cartoon figure or hand to hold them, or attention may be called to the signs with an arrow or asterisk.

Signs should be carefully worded to give information without offense. It is always best to stress the positive rather than the negative. Instead of signs saying "Do not enter," "Do not touch," or "Do not use," have signs saying "Staff only," "Please do not handle without permission," or "Consult the librarian before using these materials." If a sign says that certain materials may not be checked out, then a line should be added referring the patron to the copying machine or to similar circulating materials; "out of order" signs should direct the patron to another machine. In all cases, when a patron is told what he may not do, some directions about what he may do along the same lines should be added. This stresses the positive, which is always desirable. Every library should have a few signs posted, especially in reference areas, encouraging patrons to consult the librarian if they are unable to locate the material or information being sought.

Posters

A poster is very much like a sign in that it also gives brief information about something; the difference is that a poster is a pictorial design which tells a brief story. A poster, like most signs, requires only a few moments of attention; the message is intended to be seen and absorbed quickly. A poster is usually concerned with only one point; it should be colorful and eye-catching with a clear and direct message; and the poster and text should be large enough to be seen at a distance. A poster may publicize an important event, advertise a specific product, service, or business, or incite the reader to some specific action.

The library ordinarily uses posters only to advertise special events with which it is connected, but there are other functions, inside and outside the library, for which posters might be used. It has already been mentioned that the library should actively publicize special materials and services and should call attention to sources and types of sources; the poster would be the form most often used for this type of message. A poster may also be used to encourage the viewer to some action in which the library is directly or indirectly involved. This might include visiting the library or some section of it, voting on bond issues which might involve the library, or taking part in some community action with which the library has some connection—even if that connection involves only the supplying of relevant information.

Artistically, a poster has to be simple and direct; there is usually space and "time" to convey only one idea and this must be done with economy of effort. In terms of color all that is needed is black and white and one color—or black *or* white and two colors. There should be one dominant eye-catching shape or drawing, a very short caption, and a brief text. If details about a source or service are desired this information can be included, but the patron should be able to get the general idea without reading the details. The general idea could be the fact that an index will save time and provide needed information, and the details—which the patron need not read unless particularly interested—could furnish information on how to use an index and on the various kinds of indexes available. Some patrons, especially students, may have an immediate interest in the details; most patrons will not. Those who have noted the general message may remember it later if they need the kind of information which an index can provide; at least they have been exposed to a source which might be of use to them later.

If a number of posters are needed, it will probably be necessary to have them reproduced commercially, in which case they will be flat and two dimensional. If, however, you are making your own posters, texture and depth may be introduced; there are many ways of doing this. One effective device is to include related pamphlets as part of the design. Construction paper pamphlet holders are easy to make and they can be glued or stapled to a piece of poster board which may, in turn, be attached to the poster (the holders could be attached directly to the poster, but they would then be difficult to peel off for re-use). Pamphlet holders add an extra dimension to the poster; they can be a colorful and effective asset to the design; and, since the viewer is encouraged to touch a part of the poster, an attention-getting participation factor is added. If the poster components (cartoon, caption, and text) are on separate pieces of poster board, it is quite easy to make some of the pieces project from the surface. Any light, easily attached object will add dimension and interest, and textured materials and patterned fabrics may also be used. Anything which adds dimension, texture, or movement will make the poster more interesting and will make it easier to deliver the message which the poster conveys.

Bulletin boards

A bulletin board, technically, is a board on which notices and announcements are posted. A bulletin board is also a big problem to almost anyone having to use it. In many schools and libraries bulletin boards have been built in as part of the room decor and are of the wrong color and size and in the wrong place for display purposes; in some buildings they have been added as an afterthought and are either tiny things tucked away in corners or large, framed monsters suspended from the ceiling molding. Therefore, before a decision on form, message, or any artistic consideration can be made there is often a physical problem with which to cope.

The first step in dealing with the physical problem might be to measure all of the boards and determine whether there is too much or too little space and whether or not the space is in the most useful place. The space might consist of several very large boards in the entrance area or lobby, and scant space throughout the rest of the library; or there may be no bulletin boards in the entrance area and a plethora of bulletin board space in other areas. Or there may be ample bulletin board space everywhere, or there may be almost none at all. Almost every library has different bulletin board problems which require different solutions.

If some of the individual bulletin boards seem too large for what is usually displayed, it might be possible to have them cut down in size. In many cases, however, the decision to cut would depend on the condition of the wall behind the board; if the board has been in place a long time, the wall behind it may be in poor condition or colored differently from the surrounding area. If the size cannot be reduced physically, then it might be done artistically through use of space-filling background designs or large cartoons and captions. It might also be possible to add a wide center strip to a large board, thereby cutting it into two smaller areas which might be easier to manage for display purposes.

If additional bulletin board space is needed, perhaps more boards can be installed if there is sufficient wall space available. If the needed wall space is not available, there are a number of other space expanding solutions. Free standing boards may be purchased or made, and artists' easels can be used to hold fiberboards (if burlap is wrapped around the board and stapled to the back it will protect the soft edges of the board and obviate the need for any kind of frame). The easel display set-ups are especially useful since they take up little space and can easily be moved anywhere within or outside of the library. Boards with small, wooden supports or prop backs can be placed on tops of shelves or card catalogs; tall, narrow boards can be painted or covered with fabric and attached to the ends of book stacks; and boards may be hung from the ceiling or from balconies and used for displays on both sides. All of the boards in one area may be painted or covered with the same color to create a certain unity, or, if the library is drab, they may be in different, bright colors. These are only a few of the ways in which the available bulletin board space can be expanded or reduced; each library has to choose whatever solution is best suited to the particular situation and/or budget.

It has already been mentioned that a bulletin board is for the posting of notices. This is only one of the uses to which it can be put, but since it is the usual one, and often the messiest one, it will be considered first. The most important thing to keep in mind about notice boards is that the material, however temporary it may be, must be arranged according to some plan; it should not be tacked up helter skelter on the excuse that it will be there only a short time. The board should have a heading and/or cartoon, cutout, or some other attention getter; and if there are subdivisions of material, these should be set off in some way and should have a "lead" caption.

Notices should not be tacked directly to a bare board. The surface may be covered with a coat of paint, fabric, or construction-paper backing (use with caution since it fades and must be changed often); the covering material should be of a texture and color which will provide maximum contrast with the notices. Since the whole board will seldom be changed at one time, there should be a durable display background to make the board more attractive, more effective, and more easily used in the arrangement of temporary materials.

The first thing to be done with notices is to determine the categories into which they fall— usual subjects, usual size and shape, length of time for which they are posted—and whether there are too many of them or not enough to fill the available space. After the notices have been grouped according to subject, size, and length of stay, it will be necessary to assign priorities and space. First priority might go to notices directly relevant to the library or school, second to important community or cultural notices, and third to activities of clubs and organizations. Space should be allotted accordingly.

Since library or school notices have first priority (excluding notices of a permanent nature) they should occupy the most prominent space. If the bulletin board space is limited, they should occupy only one board; if there are several entrance boards, one should be saved, if at all possible, for a poster type of display. If one board is inadequate for the notices, the overflow could go on end-of-the-stacks boards or shelf-top stand-up boards; if there is surplus space, various kinds of space-filling designs will alleviate the problem.

In most libraries and school systems the posters and notices are usually a standard size; therefore the display background can be designed with this in mind and permanent space can be allotted. Provisions can be made to display notices side by side, or, if there are many notices, they might be arranged in layers or in overlapping "lift" patterns. If series of regular sized notices are received, acetate covers could be permanently affixed to the board and the new notices slipped into the covers. Space for posters might be sectioned off and made more noticeable by means of a cartoon figure pointing to the space; an all-purpose caption might also be used.

If clippings are often displayed for short periods of time, a definite space should be designed for them also. A cartoon figure holding his coat open could be used and clippings could be attached to the coat lining; a cartoon figure could be wearing a sandwich board to which notices could be attached; a cartoon hand might be holding a small notice board; or clippings could be displayed on a bright piece of poster board which is set off with a caption, asterisk, or arrow. The main thing to remember is that miscellaneous clippings—especially if they are of different sizes—must be brought together in some definite arrangement or confined in some definite area. If the background arrangement is set, the notices can be changed as often as necessary without disturbing it.

Permanent notices should not be displayed on the bulletin boards; it may be necessary to post them somewhere, but they are usually most unattractive and are of little immediate interest or use to most people. Depending on the number, size, and shape of the permanent notices, they can either be kept together or posted where they will do the most good as messages and the least harm as displays. They might be mounted on attractive backings and posted near the most relevant area (the fire notice near the exit and the "Not Responsible for Lost Property" warning near the coat rack), or they might all be posted on some relatively obscure board headed "For the Record."

A second priority notice board might include materials relating to jobs and training programs or to cultural events. If feasible, there should be a separate board for both types of material, but, even if there is crowding and overlapping, no more than one board each should be reserved for notices of this type. These notices are important but library business comes first. As a good will gesture some space might be allotted for posters and notices of various community happenings; if space is limited, it might be possible to provide a table-top board for typed notices of this nature. As an extra public relations gesture the notices could be color-coded with yellow asterisks or arrows tacked on for "Today's Events" and red ones for "This Week." Naturally the board should have a caption and an attention-getting device added.

In addition to the notice-posting function, a bulletin board may also be used as a large sign. This kind of sign may be used for a holiday or special week which does not rate a time-consuming display, or it may be used to point up a service or material. A particularly effective type of sign is a kind of quick quiz. For instance the library might have a series of one-question quizzes focused on subject areas (a *vejete* is (1) a little old man, (2) a jacket, (3) a type of house—an added note will mention that Spanish-language books and dictionaries are in the 463's); on services (Framed prints are loaned for A, B, or C weeks); or on materials (This library has A, B, or C number of books). Be sure that the answer is posted nearby. Different series of quizzes could be prepared and then used for a few days while the display is being changed. Any sign board ought to begin with a good design background; the sign should be large and effectively lettered; and each sign should be displayed for only a few days at a time.

A bulletin board may also serve as a poster, and, used in this way, is subject to all of the rules applying to posters. The main advantages which a bulletin board poster has over a regular poster are the usually larger size, the more prominent placement, and the fact that it is easier to use fabric, 3-D devices, and other objects on it. It is much easier to attach items such as pamphlet holders, book jackets or books, and other objects to a bulletin board than to a poster. This relative ease of attachment also means that bulletin boards can often be used for displays and exhibits.

Displays and exhibits

Display and exhibit have almost identical meanings and both terms are used as both nouns and verbs. A further complication in pinning down the meaning is the fact that the plurals of the words are often used to refer to the whole range of visual publicity. In practice a display is usually a bit more limited in scope than an exhibit, but there is no definite dividing line. In a narrower sense both terms refer to arranging objects in such a way that we see the object itself and also the connective idea which ties the individual items together; there has to be some theme or message behind the organization of materials. The display or exhibit might show progression or growth, or aspects or views of a subject; it may be limited to a particular medium or form, to a geographic area, to a period of time, or to a subject of study.

If the materials are two dimensional or not too heavy, they can be displayed on one or several bulletin boards. Objects may be shown on shelves attached to the board or suspended by wire or cord. Large displays, or displays involving both two- and three-dimensional items, might utilize bulletin boards and also tables or display cases. A display of any kind usually requires special arrangements in terms of gathering the materials, grouping them in a coherent manner, and arranging suitable space. There is also the problem of making the display effective and attractive. The arrangement must be logical and clear; there must be sufficient labels; and design principles must be adhered to.

It was mentioned at the beginning of this chapter that all of these forms—signs, posters, bulletin boards, and displays—are overlapping and that in practice the distinctions between them often disappear. It is impossible to assign priorities and to say that any one of them is more important in a library than any other. All of them should be considered in the over-all display program, and one kind of message should not always be restricted to the same form. The messages and the forms are mix and match components, and for maximum results the message should be delivered through as many different channels or forms as possible; there is a fairly wide selection from which to choose and the leeway for experimentation is almost unlimited.

5. Design elements and principles

The time has come to get down to the basics of display technique—design elements and principles. There is nothing to be leery of since most people have been using these basics for years even though they may not have been aware of it; each time a person straightens a picture, tidies his desk, or moves a pillow or chair to a different location he is applying some kind of order (design principle) and the object which was moved or rearranged is a design element. In display work a bulletin board is a shape and notices or whatever one puts on it are design elements; and a completed board, good or bad, is a design. Various shortcuts to good design are discussed in chapter 6. Here, we will begin with the basic elements: color, line, shape, texture, and space.

Color

Since color is an important and indispensable tool for anyone preparing displays, the various qualities and uses of color must be mentioned. Many of the potentials of color may be left unexploited, but one should know about them for they will affect art work whether or not they are used consciously. Therefore, we will briefly review some of the technical and psychological aspects of color before discussing their practical applications.

For practical purposes it is probably easiest to define color as a hue as distinct from black, white, and gray. Two of the commonly recognized properties or qualities of color are *value*, which refers to the relative lightness or darkness of a color, and *chroma*, or *intensity*, which refers to the relative strength or weakness of a color. Value is further subdivided into *tints*, or *pastels*, which applies to colors to which white has been added; and *shades*, which means colors to which black has been added. These terms may seem somewhat confusing at first, but the discussion should clarify their meaning.

There are three primary colors, yellow, blue, and red; and these colors are mixed in various proportions to produce all the other colors (this concept relates only to "flat" colors and not to light rays, to which an entirely different color theory applies). When mixed in equal proportions these primary colors produce the secondary colors; yellow and blue make green, blue and red make purple, and red and yellow make orange. The six intermediate colors are produced with one primary color (which is named first) dominating in the mixture; they are yellow-green, blue-green, blue-purple, red-purple, red-orange, and yellow-orange. These are the generic, operating names but we usually encounter the colors under various fashion pseudonyms. In display work the thing to remember is that all of these colors are mixed from the primary colors of yellow, blue, and red; and that if we add white to any of these colors, we have tints; and if we add black, we have shades.

The color wheel (see frontispiece) shows these colors in their correct "mixing" relationship, and this wheel is used to determine the various types of color harmony. The color harmony which will be of most use in display work is the one involving *complementary* colors; complementary colors are those which are opposite each other on the color wheel. When placed side by side complementary colors intensify each other; they are seldom used together in equal amounts since this divides attention, but a touch of orange used with blue will add snap to any display — and the same applies to red and green, yellow and purple, blue-purple and yellow-orange, and any of the other combinations of complementary colors. Another useful fact to know about complementary colors is that when they are mixed together in equal amounts, they produce a neutral gray; therefore, if one is mixing colors and wishes to tone one down slightly without dulling it (as the addition of black would do), it can be done by means of the addition of a

very small amount of the complementary color.

Another type of color relationship is *monochromatic* harmony, which consists of tints and shades of one color. This harmony is too subtle for most display purposes, but it is often used in interior decoration. An *analogous* color harmony is made up of colors (usually three) which are side-by-side on the color wheel: blue-green, blue, and blue-purple would constitute an analogous harmony. Any of these three harmonies can be used alone or in combination; for instance, a monochromatic or analogous harmony based on blue can be enlivened by adding a touch of the complementary color, orange.

In addition to properties and harmonies, there are two other important aspects of color to be considered: colors can advance and recede (visually), and colors have certain psychological connotations. Red, red-orange, and yellow are often spoken of as "warm" colors, and blue, blue-green, and purple as "cool" colors. The warm colors seem to advance toward the observer and the cool colors to recede; intense colors also advance, and shades and tints recede. The applications of these factors to display work are rather obvious; seasonal displays should make use of colors appropriate to the temperature, and, in general, the intense, warm colors which seem to advance are more effective for posters than are the cool colors, and the tints and shades.

The warm and cool colors are, in part, the result of a psychological reaction (the warm colors suggest sun and fire, and cool colors suggest water and snow), but colors also have other inherent or acquired psychological meanings in addition to temperature. Green is restful; blue suggests melancholy; black is gloomy; white has connotations of purity, etc.; then there are groups of colors which have acquired certain connotations, such as red and green for stop and go; and red, white, and blue for patriotism. These associations of certain feelings with certain colors are rather generally accepted, but there are also individual reactions to color which negate the supposed group response. Reliance on these psychological factors can be useful in display work, but, since individual response is often variable, one should not place too much faith in the psychological aspects of color.

Now we will cover somewhat the same ground in strictly practical terms. Use intense colors and avoid the use of tints unless there is a definite reason for doing so. Limit displays to black and white (or tan) and one intense color, with a slight preference for warm colors which seem to advance. Order construction paper and poster board of good quality since the colors will usually have more intensity than those of cheaper materials. Try to avoid ordering assortments which have a high proportion of tints (most do); it would be better to order single packs of only a few intense colors and black and white than to be burdened with the tints. If ordering is done through a central service try to make arrange-

ments to acquire only what you need and want.

Use strong contrasts: light and dark, high and low intensity, and warm and cool colors. Boards should be either light or dark in color. Stark white as a background is often too glaring, but off-white or tan is quite effective and materials such as natural burlap, grasscloth, or matchstick bamboo make excellent coverings for your boards. Though it may seem surprising (since black is supposed to have gloomy connotations), a matte (not glossy) black makes a highly effective background; light and intense colors spring to life against a black board. Furthermore, since most signs and display elements will be light in color, a black background will provide an automatic contrast.

Use dark accents on a light board and light accents on a dark one; use light, dark, light or dark, light, dark. This is not as vague as it may sound; it simply means that if the board is light and the display materials are also light (light-toned book jackets for instance), something dark should be put between the background and the display materials. If the background and display materials are both dark tones, then something light is needed to separate them — a sheet of white or yellow poster board or a piece of natural burlap.

In establishing strong contrast, white, tan, and black are your chief allies. When planning a board or display it is best to think of it only in terms of light, dark, and one color. Another color may be added later, but if initial planning includes only one color the result will usually be a simpler and more effective design. In most cases one color will be all that is needed, but a spot of the complementary color may be added for heightened effect. Remember at all times that good design is usually simple design; adding many colors will not disguise a poor design and it will usually add clutter rather than effect.

Line

Line is the second basic element in display work, and for anyone doing displays line has at least four different meanings and uses. For one thing, a line is a long mark which may be thick, thin, curved, or broken. This kind of line may be used to direct the eye or to wrap up an area as string does a package; in fact, use string, use rope, use wide strips of paper. Use a broken line; rectangles or squares of paper (dark if they are to be used on a light surface, and light if on dark) used in a row are much more effective than a solid line would be.

These lines can move across a surface to direct the eye where you wish it to go—to another part of the design, to a block of text, or to a display item or object. They can also wrap up groups of items in order to relate them to one another and separate them from the rest of the design. For example, black or white rug yarn can be used to "wrap up" a group of notices or book jackets; this device will tie the various elements together in a design sense (they will become a square or rectangle of design rather than a group of miscellaneous materials) and will set them off and make them more important. As with colors, certain lines have certain psychological effects. Horizontal lines suggest solidity and repose; vertical lines suggest strength; diagonal lines are dynamic, and curved lines are suggestive of movement. Repetition of a line reinforces the feeling it suggests, and crossing lines create an area of high interest where the lines intersect.

A line is also the edge where two shapes meet; two sheets of paper placed side by side have a "line" between them; if one sheet is smaller and is placed on top of the other, there is a contour line around the edge of the smaller sheet. A line is also a row of things: a row of circles, a row of book jackets, a row of notices. This row can function in much the same way as a drawn or painted line; it can lead the eye along and it elicits the same psychological reactions—a vertical arrangement will suggest strength, a diagonal arrangement will be dynamic, and so on. All of these lines have to be "aimed"; they should not be scattered about at random and they should not shoot off in diverse directions. You have to decide what part of your design is most important and then reinforce it and direct attention to it by judicious use of line; since you have a variety of different lines from which to choose, select the ones most appropriate to your purpose.

There is one other line which can play a large

part in your design; it is an invisible line which might be called a margin line. A page of print has a definite margin at top, bottom, and sides, and if there are illustrations they are lined up in accord with this margin; this edge line is a very important part of the page layout. Since this margin is not drawn in — except by your eye — it is an invisible line. A bulletin board, poster or display has the same kind of invisible line involved in the layout, and an effort should be made to have a margin on at least two sides of the design. In most cases a four-sided margin would be impossible because of the diverse size and shape of the display materials; but the bottom row of items could be aligned along the lower edge, and the items could be aligned at the right.

There should also be some margin lines within the design: the bottom of a cartoon could be in line with the top or bottom of a block of print or a row of display items; a caption could be in line at the top with the top of a cartoon and the left side could be in line with other items displayed; any kind of row should be in line with something else in the design. The more items to be displayed the more need there is for these invisible lines; without them the design will look like a hodge podge. Attention to line does not mean that all the elements in the design must be lined up — they need not — but some things must be. The board should be designed with that principle kept in mind, or a tentative arrangement of materials should be made and the elements moved around as re-

quired in order to achieve the essential margins.

Shape

The third element is shape; a shape is a form — round, square, big, little, regular, or irregular. The bulletin board itself is a shape, usually a rectangle. Everything which is put on it is a shape; the design elements chosen may be of any shape but the printed items are almost always rectangles. The chief problem is to arrange all of the different size and shape items into larger and more important shapes and then to relate them to the rest of the design.

The first thing to remember about background shapes is to keep them large and simple. Stick to the basic shapes of squares, rectangles, circles, triangles, and so forth, for background. For special emphasis use variations on punctuation-mark shapes such as an asterisk, question mark, or exclamation point; these are clean-cut shapes with built-in meaning and emphasis — they are also good design. Avoid free forms such as amorphous, cloudlike shapes; they are usually just fillers and detract from rather than add to the design. Make large and bold shapes with simple contour lines; use as few shapes as possible and do not use two or three small shapes where one large one could be used.

The second thing to remember about shapes is not to mix them too much: rectangles and squares are usually unavoidable; therefore, if possible, use only one other shape. Use one large triangle or three adjoining or overlapping triangles (odd numbers are more interesting than even, so when repeating a shape, do so twice rather than once); use one or three large circles as a background and then smaller circles for emphasis within the design. Try to limit the different sizes used; as a general rule, use only two sizes of the same shape, and make the difference in size extreme.

Texture

Element number four is texture: texture is the visual or tactile appearance of a surface. Surfaces can look or feel smooth, rough, soft, hard, cool, or warm; they can look pleasant or unpleasant to touch. Certain combinations of texture have special appeal; smooth and rough, cool and warm, natural and man-made. You mix textures in your home; a nubby material on a couch against a smooth wall, a furry rug on a polished floor, wood grain against a brick wall, and fragile curtains against rough textured drapes. Your house would be dull if there were no contrast in surface texture; the same applies to a display or bulletin board.

Use smooth poster board against natural burlap; make use of rough textured paper or vinyl backgrounds; use fabric, corrugated cardboard (but beware of insipid tints), grasscloth beach mats, textured place mats (especially good for displaying photographs), and yarn and rope for line. Natural fabrics and textures are especially good for backgrounds because they have a high recognition factor (we know how they feel) and provide texture contrast with any paper object displayed against them. Since most printed material has no tactile quality, texture is an especially valuable and striking ingredient for made-to-order displays; even a poor design will look better with the addition of texture.

Space

The fifth and last element is space. Space is depth, the third dimension, objects that are in front of or behind other things — or around them, or projecting from them. Space adds interest, excitement, and contrast to your design. It is also easy to add. Plan the board "flat" and then look at it in terms of space; how would it look if that circle, square, or caption projected a bit? Project it. A small item can be projected by attaching it to a small cardboard box and then attaching the box to the display, and there are also easy methods of folding cardboard or poster board which will give you a 3-D effect. Even more simple, any shape which overlaps another seems to be in front of it; and warm colors, as we have already mentioned, seem to be in front of cool ones. If one is using a cartoon figure, it is easy to make an arm and hand project from the board; if the hand is holding something, so much the better. An object can be displayed easily by constructing a shelf and attaching it to the bulletin board. Anything which adds depth or appearance of depth will add to the effectiveness of a display

There you have it; those are all of the elements of design: color, line, shape, texture, and space. We now go on to a few of the mix and match rules for using them; the rules are simplicity, emphasis, unity and balance.

Simplicity

Simplicity is clearness and lack of complication. It is use of only a few colors or black and white and one color; it is use of only one or two basic shapes and only one or two different sizes of these shapes; it is simple organization of your materials. It is clearness and economy in selection of the idea or ideas to be sold; if an attempt is made to sell too much at one time, nothing will be sold. Stick to one or two ideas or products at a time. In essence: choose only one or two ideas or products to sell; tell a minimum about them; be economical in the selection of color as well as of shape and texture; and organize the materials as simply as possible.

Emphasis

Emphasis is the stress or prominence given to an idea or design element. It is making one idea, color, shape, or texture dominant and others subordinate; if all of these elements are of equal interest, no one of them will receive attention. Emphasize only the dominant idea or shape by making it larger, brighter, more textured; surround it with empty space, lead into it with lines, point to it with a fat arrow, make it project from

the board. Every design has to have one main center of interest if it is to make a point; there may be secondary items and areas of interest but these should not compete with the central idea. A center of interest in terms of idea must be chosen; then design elements must be utilized to make it the center of design interest.

Unity

One definition of unity is "singleness of effect or style"; another is "totality of related parts." In display work unity is often a simple matter of repetition and consistency. It is the overlapping of three identical shapes in different colors; it is use of a large square and a few smaller ones elsewhere in the design; it is use of any shape, color, line, or texture with a repeat of it elsewhere in the design. It is the repetition of similar elements in a different size or color. It is consistency in the style of lettering. Each of the elements in any design should mesh with every other element and should relate to the whole so that a single effect is achieved.

Balance

The dictionary defines balance as a "weight, force, or influence countering the effect of another." This is acceptable as a starting point, but the real problem is in determining the visual weight of various design elements; some textures and colors weigh more than others in a design sense, and this visual weight varies depending on the environment. Balance in a design is achieved when the visual weight of the elements on one side of a display is equal to the visual weight of the elements on the other side. The elements can be divided equally to create formal balance, or a trickier and more effective informal balance can be attempted (informal balance is based more on arrangement than on actual weight). Formal balance is much easier to determine and handle so it is particularly recommended when there are many items to be displayed; when working with a single idea or item, informal balance is often the better solution. Balance is something which really has to be seen, and the illustrations in this book point out various kinds and applications of balance.

6. Design components

It was mentioned earlier that there are some shortcuts to good design. These shortcut techniques are not intended to eliminate planning publicity in advance, nor are they a substitute for creative designing of bulletin boards and displays. They are simplified design techniques to assist in planning displays and to help in achieving maximum results with minimum time and effort. The fact that many of these techniques are simple, adaptable, and reasonably foolproof is due to their being based on design principles and effective advance planning.

The first two techniques, which are separate but related, are the use of simple, geometric shapes and the use of positive and negative space. The latter technique undoubtedly requires some explanation and that, perhaps, can best be done by describing the process. Suppose that a circle is cut from the middle of a piece of poster board; the circle should be centered and if the board is the usual 22- by 28-inch size the diameter of the circle should be about 16 or 17 inches. The circle must be cut in such a way that the background is left in one piece (if a "cut-in" is made the edges can be taped together from the back). The cutout circle is a positive shape and the hole left in the piece of poster board is a negative shape. Placed side by side, the positive and negative shapes produce an instant design background which is both simple and effective.

This positive-negative technique can be used with any shape but it is usually most effective with common geometric shapes and with large arrows and asterisks. If some of the same shapes are cut in different sizes and colors, both the positive and negative shapes can be used in different combinations; to add variety, some of the forms could also be covered with burlap or other printed or textured fabrics. At least a few of the shapes should be cut in the largest possible size which can be used on the library bulletin boards. Poster board and construction paper can be purchased in large sizes, and it might also be possible to have some of the shapes cut from 4- by 8-foot sheets of fiber board. One might start with only a few shapes but these should be added to as time and the budget permit; the more there are on hand, the easier it should be to design displays.

Examples of a few shapes and ways in which they can be employed might help clarify the potential usefulness of these techniques. Figure 1 shows an example of positive and negative shapes designed to fill most of the space on a bulletin board. Figures 2 through 5 are examples of ways in which the same design background can be used for different displays. Figure 6 shows the circle combined with another positive shape for a similar kind of quick display. Figure 7 pictures rectangular positive and negative shapes, and Figures 8 through 12 illustrate some of the different arrangements and varying uses to which the shapes can be put. Here, too, the shapes were cut large enough to fill most of the space and also to provide a background for displaying book jackets or books.

An ellipse is shown in Figure 13 and the illustrations following suggest some of the ways in which this very adaptable shape might be used. Figures 13 and 14 are general background designs which could be used for the same types of displays shown for the circular backgrounds. The design in Figure 15 suggests a tree shape and it might be used for a bulletin board directing attention to fall reading. Figures 16 through 19 show some stylized faces; captions might tell the viewer to "See" or "Look at" a book display, new equipment, improvement, or exhibit; or to "Watch for" some service or program offered by the library. In Figures 20 and 21 triangular tails and round eyes have turned the ellipses into fish. The first design might be used with such captions as "Get in the Swim" or "Get Hooked on Books" (a fishing line and hook could be added);

captions for the second fish design might be "Bring the Family" or "Follow the Crowd." Figure 22 is made of a combination of ellipses and one circle, and captions might direct attention to spring or summer reading or to books on gardening.

Rectangles are usually less interesting than other shapes, but they can be useful for displaying certain types of materials. Rectangles are a particularly effective background when the items to be displayed are either numerous or of differing sizes; the psychologically stable shape of a rectangle seems to help pull multiple or diverse objects into a unified whole. Figure 23 shows three rectangles and Figure 24 has added more background interest by having one of the shapes cut in half. Figure 25 shows how this type of background might be put to use; additional interest has been added with a caption that projects slightly. A "before" board showing how notices might look without a background is shown in Figure 26. In Figure 27 the appearance of the board is improved by the addition of two rectangles; Figure 28 is improved still further with the addition of a 3-D caption. (Lettering techniques will be discussed in Chapter 7, but Figure 29 indicates the steps involved in lettering a simple caption.) Before and after views of another notice board are shown in Figures 30 and 31.

The discussion has covered only a few of the combinations and uses of geometric shapes and

1

2

3

4

5

6

7

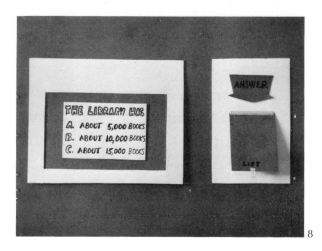

THE LIBRARY HAS
A. ABOUT 5,000 BOOKS
B. ABOUT 10,000 BOOKS
C. ABOUT 15,000 BOOKS

ANSWER

LIFT

8

PUT QUOTATION HERE

9

WHITMAN

10

HAVE YOU SEEN OUR NEW BOOKS?

11

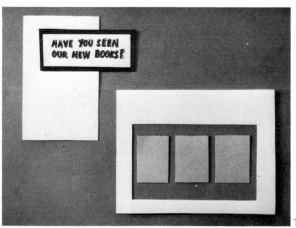

HAVE YOU SEEN OUR NEW BOOKS?

12

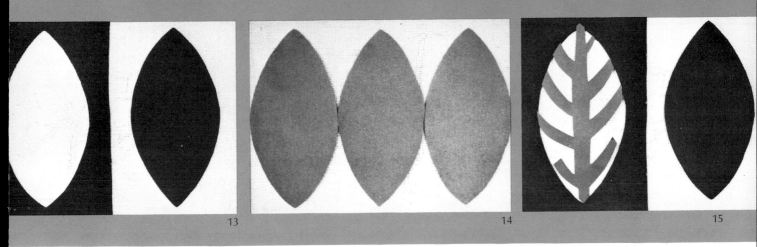

13

14

15

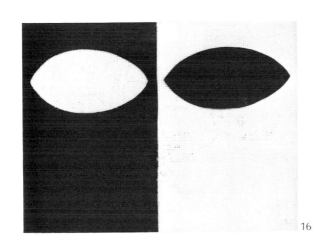

16

17

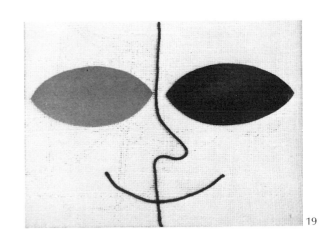

18

19

20

21

22

23

24

25

26

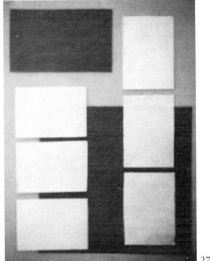

27

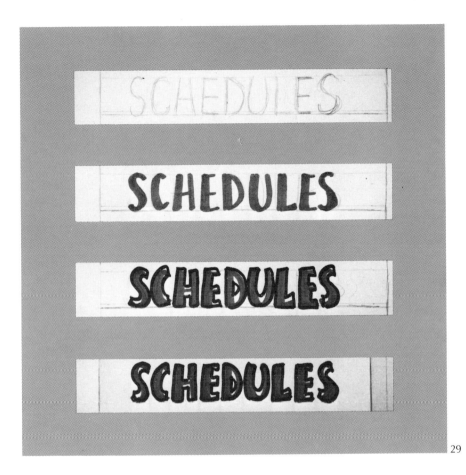

29

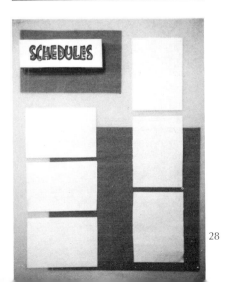

28

30

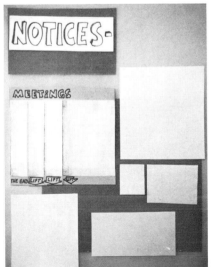

31

of positive and negative space, but the subject is almost endless. The purpose has been to indicate rather than to delineate the design possibilities. Use of almost any geometric shape, particularly if it is repeated, will help to add unity to a design and the shape will often suggest design motifs (plants, animals, and objects); the motifs, in turn, may suggest captions and display materials.

The advantages of this type of display are multiple. Any time a rush display is needed, one need only select a few basic ingredients (background shapes) and add a dash of spice (caption, comment, quotation, reproduction, phonograph album cover, and so forth). Bulletin boards can be kept fresh with minimum effort if the background design is retained and the "spice" changed often. When it is time for a complete change of scene, a new set of basic ingredients can be selected and the old ones stored for future use. Other elements may be added to make the design even more effective: shapes can be raised to add dimension; texture, lift panels, pamphlet holders, yarn or rope can be added; and appropriate objects can be included. It should be remembered, however, that indiscriminate additions will only detract from the effectiveness of the display; no more than one or two extras should be added to any basic design.

Preparation of cartoon and caption assortments is another technique which reduces the time needed to assemble individual displays. The main requirement of this technique is creative, long-range planning. It must be decided which cartoons and captions are most useful and how they can be combined most effectively. Here too, size is very important; most of the cartoons should cover from one fourth to one half of the background space on which they are to be used, and the captions should be almost as large. Different sizes will probably be required for bulletin boards, posters, and desk- or shelf-top stand-up displays. Some of the cartoons which will be suggested are simple enough to be copied by almost anyone; others might require the skills of an art student or professional.

Figure 32 is a man with a head full of reading suggestions. Some of the possible captions which might accompany him are "Which Type of Reading Do You Like?" "May We Offer Some Suggestions?" "We Cater to All Reading Tastes" "May We Help You Choose?" and "Try Something New in Reading." The display might include book jackets, or photocopies of book jackets, representing all of the listed reading ideas; bright colored circles with numbers could be added near each reading type and corresponding numbers placed with the appropriate book jacket. One might also display only one type of reading material at a time. A large, bright asterisk might be placed next to "Biography," and only books of that genre would be displayed; then the asterisk could be moved and another type of reading could be featured. If the featured books were changed weekly, one would, with very little effort, have a different display for seven consecutive weeks.

You can use No. 32 for other types of displays simply by giving his brain a new poster board cover. His brain might contain types of reference books or library services with specific information about sources and services shown elsewhere on the board, names of authors to be matched with book titles listed on the board, or dates to be matched with authors or books. When 32 is used for matching quizzes, numbers and letters should be used and the answer should be on the same board or posted nearby.

Figure 33 is a frightened-looking fellow, so he might be used with captions which tell him, "Don't Be Scared," "Don't Be Shy," "It Doesn't Bite," "It Won't Hurt to Try," or "Aw, Come on and Use It." He can be used to introduce information about the library in general, library services, types of sources, or reading or copying machines. He might also be told to "Cheer Up" with certain kinds of reading material or he might be offered "Mysteries for People Who Like to Be Scared."

Figure 34 is obviously ready for a trip. He can be used to offer books on travel or books to be read "While You Travel," "Before You Travel" or "After You Get Back"; he could be encouraged to "Travel at Home" or to "Take Some Paperbacks" or to "Remember Our Summer-Loan

Plan." He might also be used to tell patrons about the foreign-language books or records. Figure 34 could be made more interesting with the addition of a fabric hat and/or clothing, a real pair of dark glasses, and a few travel stickers on his luggage.

Figure 35 seems to be deep in thought or worried about something. He might be told, "Don't Be So Glum," "It Can't Be That Bad," "Things Will Get Better," "We Didn't Do It On Purpose," or "We Know It's Confusing." He can be very useful in presenting explanations or apologies about library services or policies— operating hours, book checks at the door, fines, closed stacks, lack of space, repair work, problems of understaffing, microfilming of materials, interlibrary loans, and so on. He might also be used to describe such procedures as applying for a library card; he could be given directions about the use of various machines in the library; or the library budget could be explained to him. He could also be directed to reference sources which might help him solve his problems or to reading materials which might help to cheer him up.

Figure 36 has something to show or to tell about. His coat lining could be used to show titles of new books, names of reference books, lists of services, or book lists and reviews. He might also be giving the patron "Inside Info" on a service or special program. Attention might be attracted with "Pssssst," "Hot Tips for Good

Reading," "Latest Info," "Hot off the Press," "Check This," or "For Insiders Only." Since most notices and signs are light in color, the coat lining should be dark in order to provide contrast. The lining could be of fabric and buttons could be used on the outside.

Figure 37 looks as though he might have just had a very bright idea, and a light bulb (real or cutout) might be attached above his head to emphasize it. His idea could be about a kind of reading material, a particular source, a program he wishes to attend, an exhibit he has just remembered, or a change of hours he has almost forgotten about. He might be saying, "I Just Remembered," "I Mustn't Forget," "I Almost Forgot," "That's What I Need," or "That's Where I Should Look." Or he might be told, "Don't Forget," "Mark That Down," "Be Sure to Remember," "We Want to Remind You," or "Have You Thought of ...?"

Figure 38 can be adjusted to accommodate almost any kind of notice. He can be made in a large size and used on a bulletin board or he can be propped up and used as a 12-inch-high stand atop a desk. Since he will probably be holding a light-colored notice, he should either be cut out and mounted on dark-colored poster board or shown holding a dark piece of board to which light-colored notices may be attached. He will add importance and attractiveness to almost any notice, even a hastily scribbled one (and, because most people write better than they print, a hasty notice usually looks better if it is written—with a marking pen for clarity and legibility). If the hands of the cartoon figure are cut out entirely, they may be moved around on the display board and used to hold almost anything from the top, bottom, or sides. In addition to notices, the figure might be holding a book jacket, a map (to promote travel books), a pamphlet holder, a checkerboard (to publicize books on games), or almost anything else that is of the right size and that can be easily attached to a poster or bulletin board.

Figure 39 shows two kinds of cartoon hands which can have multiple uses in display work. The "holding" hand can be used almost anywhere in the library to call attention to directions or procedures. If the cartoon hand is drawn life size, it can be mounted to poster board and propped on desks and shelves, or it can be attached to bookcases, cabinets, windows, etc. If the thumb of the cartoon hand is left unglued, notices may easily be slipped underneath it. The pointing hand can direct attention to almost anything which might be of interest to the patron; it too may be used almost anywhere in the library. Both types of hands may be drawn extra large for use on bulletin boards or on book trucks. And, for the sake of variety and attractiveness, the hands could be drawn or painted on poster boards of various colors.

These are only a few suggestions for mix-and-match components, but the cartoons and cap-

CARTOON HANDS CAN HOLD SIGNS OR POINT OUT DIRECTIONS

tions mentioned form a basic kind of display repertory company. One need only assemble the members and assign roles and captions. Other cartoons and captions should of course be added, and each addition will increase the flexibility and effectiveness of any display program.

Now all that the repertory company needs is a few stage props—large poster-board cutouts. Almost all cutouts should be as large as possible and simple in outline; details, texture, and dimension may be added later, but the basic form must be simple and clean-cut. Figure 40 shows a basic cutout of a bus and Figure 41 shows the same bus with a few additions. One might also add wheels from a child's construction set, aluminum foil "chrome" strips, or cartoon faces in the windows. Captions used might be "Everyone's Coming," "On the Move Again," "Load Up—With Good Reading," "Travel Through Books," "Take a Trip Through Story Land," or "Books to Pack Along."

A house cutout is shown in Figure 42, and Figure 43 shows how it might look after some design rehabilitation. Attic and door windows and window sills have been added, I-shaped cuts in the windows have been opened out to make shutters, and a backing sheet of white paper provides window panes. The basic shape has not been changed. Figure 44 has added dimension to the house; a small square of poster board has been used to make the attic project and another folded piece of poster board has been attached to make a projecting front step. Among other things which might be added are acetate windows, brick or wood-textured siding, balsa wood shutters, a poster-board window box. (In a school library it is often a good idea to let students make additions to cutout shapes.) This kind of cutout could offer "Reading for Stay-at-Homes," "Tips for Homemakers," "Home Repair Ideas," "How to Buy a House," or "Hobbies for Housewives."

Use of geometric shapes as design motifs was mentioned earlier in this chapter. These shapes can often be combined with other cutouts or cartoons to create striking displays. Some of the possible combinations:

1. A bulletin board could be covered with large black squares in a checkerboard pattern, with cutouts of checker or chess pieces, and appropriate captions to direct attention to books on games or sports. Captions such as "It's Your Move," "Plan Your Strategy," and "Don't Get Cornered" might also be used to promote materials on schools and careers, investments, and consumer education, and how-to-do-it books.

2. A cartoon man could be shown carried "Up, Up and Away" by three large circle balloons (see Figure 45). He might be offered various kinds of escape reading and travel books, or he could be directed to books to solve his problems and make his flight unnecessary ("Is This Flight Really Necessary?"). Other possible captions are "Travel (or Take Off) With Books" and "Flights of Fancy," which might be used with fairy tales.

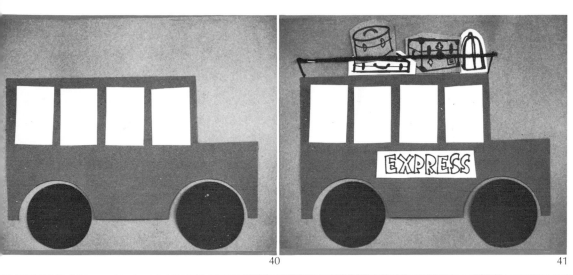

40

41

42

43

44

45

3. A cartoon figure shown "Behind the 8-Ball" could be offered various kinds of escape reading to help take his mind off his problems, or the display might suggest materials to help solve his problems.

4. A cartoon figure could be "Boxed In" by three large squares and he too could be offered materials to boost his morale or to help him out of his dilemma.

Naturally all of these props should be carefully dismantled and stored along with the backgrounds, characters, and captions. All items from the publicity repertory company should be stage ready at any time so repairing, refurbishing, and replacing should be constant. Since most display ideas are old, the ingredients should be new, at least in appearance.

And it must be admitted that none of the display ideas in this chapter are entirely new; most of them are adaptations or new combinations of rather standard ingredients—but that, for the most part, is what display work is all about. Any or all of the ideas presented may be imitated (but not reproduced) to help you get started or adapted to help you keep going. It is best to remember that there are few, if any, entirely new ideas, and that it is impossible to make each display new and different. But it is possible to make each display fresh and imaginative and that should be the goal of anyone doing displays.

7. Lettering, layout, and cartooning

Many people regard lettering as one of the most difficult and frustrating aspects of display work. Much of this frustration is due to the commonly held belief that plain, simple letters should be the easiest to execute and that if one cannot draw them adequately there is absolutely no point in attempting other kinds of letters. It is true that lettering, even among commercial artists, is a specialty requiring long hours of study and practice. But it is also true that the thin, straight, and seemingly simple lettering attempted by most amateurs is actually the most difficult to do free-hand, without a ruler or some other mechanical aid. No attempt will be made to teach this kind of "simple" lettering. If one has a facility for lettering, it is worth while to develop it; but if one is rather inept, and most of us are in that category, it is more expedient to learn only a few, adaptable types of freehand lettering and to rely on lettering kits and prepared letters for variety.

The easiest, fastest, and most adaptable lettering for an amateur is a type which involves combining two rather sloppy kinds of letters: a simple painted letter and an outline letter executed with a felt marking pen. The technique employed to produce these letters is very sim-

ple; the materials required are the following:
a flat brush at least 1/4-inch in width;
a black felt marking pen with a wide tip;
poster paint, preferably red, blue, or green;
a number of 2- or 3-inch strips of white poster board.

The brush should be loaded with paint, and, with the flat of the brush, a word or phrase should be printed on a strip of poster board (paper should not be used since it tends to curl when paint is applied). The letters should be "fat" and "juicy." They may be sloppy and uneven but that is not important; it is important, however, to keep the letters simple, with no extra curves or curlicues. Figure 46 shows how this type of letter might look; if lettering is shaggier than the example, that is unimportant. Since the paint has to dry thoroughly before the second step, it might be best to paint a number of practice strips at one time. When lettering is being done for a sign or poster, it is best to pencil in the text and margin lines, but that is not necessary for a practice session.

Step two, after the painted letters have dried, is to outline the letters with a marking pen. The full width of the tip should be used in order to make a broad outline, and one may also use the wide side of the marker for an even wider line. No attempt should be made to outline the letters exactly; outlining should be done quickly and loosely with some overlapping of the painted letters and some gaps. Figure 47 shows the kind of outline letter to be used, and Figure 48 shows how the two types of letters look in combination. What has been done is to combine two kinds of casual (or sloppy) letters to achieve an easy and effective kind of display letter.

This type of letter might also be made with two felt markers, one colored and one black. The colored marker can be used in place of the paint and extra strokes can make the letter wider. Marking-pen letters are shown in Figure 49, and Figure 50 shows them outlined. Since marking ink dries instantly, this is a faster method than painting the letters. Paint, however, is more intense in color than are the inks in marking pens; and, since any size paint brush may be used, there can be greater flexibility in letter size. Using paint for the basic letter is usually worth the extra effort, but it is a matter of personal choice.

Different effects may be achieved by varying the materials and techniques slightly. Outline letters may be used alone as in Figure 51. Using outline letters is often not so simple as it looks; at first, one tends to get "lost" and lose the shape of the letter. After outlining solid letters for a time, however, it becomes much easier to make the outline letters separately. The letters may also be shaded slightly to make them look three-dimensional; that may be done with the outline letters alone or with the combination letters (see Figure 52). Black marking pens are usually most effective for outlining, but there may be occasions when another color would be preferred; one could use blue paint and a blue marker, blue paint and a red marker, or any other combination that may be desired. Some marking pens have washable inks but indelible colors are preferable because the color is usually more intense and more lasting.

Another advantage of combination letters is that they can be made as large or small as one wishes. For small letters, a very small pointed brush can be used for the painting (sable brushes are more expensive but they last longer, hold a point better, and shed hairs less than the cheaper bristle brushes); and a fine-tipped fiber pen may be used for the outlining. Larger letters require the use of the broad side of a wide, flat brush and the broad side of a felt marker. This kind of letter may also be compressed or expanded to meet individual needs; examples of this are shown in Figures 53 and 54. Figure 55 pictures still another variation achieved by means of a dry brush and rather dry poster paint.

Cutout letters are also very useful for display purposes. Here too, amateurs often attempt to make the thin, straight letters which are the most difficult to do. The thinner the cutout letter, the more difficult it is to keep straight and of even thickness, and the harder it is to handle. The

POSTER 46

POSTER 47

POSTER 48

POSTER 49

POSTER 50

POSTER 51

POSTER 52

POSTER 53

POSTER 54

POSTER 55

POSTER 56

POSTER 57

POSTER 58

letters in Figure 56 have been carefully cut but there are still variations in thickness and regularity. If cutout letters are as broad and blocky as possible (see Figure 57), they are easier to cut and to handle, and they are also more effective for displays. All letters except I can be cut from the same size square or rectangle, and the absolute minimum of paper should be cut away. The "holes" may be skipped entirely or they may be punched out later with a small ring punch, and, in that case, only one ring hole should be punched in a letter regardless of the letter size. The production of cutout letters is one of the few processes for which construction paper is preferable to the heavier poster board, which is difficult to cut with scissors.

Dark letters should be used on a light board and light letters should be used on a dark board. One very simple trick that achieves attractive results is to switch the dark-light arrangement in the middle of a word or phrase. If, for example, one half of the display is black and the other half is yellow, the lettering can be designed to cross from the yellow to the black background. Black letters would be used against the yellow, and yellow letters would be used against the black (see Figure 58).

There are many advantages in being able to do one's own lettering: after a bit of practice, hand lettering (with the exception of cutout letters) is usually faster than most other methods; one is able to choose the exact size and color desired;

lettering kits are often short of needed letters and letters are often broken, bent, or discolored; and handmade letters can be much more attractive and effective than commercial letters. There are, of course, many times when lettering kits can be of use. Mitten letters (plaster letters with sharp, wire prongs) are very useful for bulletin boards because of the 3-D element; and cardboard glue-on letters are also useful but are less effective and less durable. There are various types of press-on letters which come in sheets; these are good for small signs, but care must be taken to keep the letters in even rows. There are also mechanical aids which help one to do very neat and legible lettering: a Leroy set makes pen-and-ink lettering almost foolproof if time is taken in learning to use it properly. Stencil letters should be avoided; they are messy to use and the result is usually uneven and unattractive.

One very useful technique, and one which can be used with freehand or commercial letters, is to make or place the letters on strips of poster board. One must estimate the space to be filled and the amount of text and then cut strips of poster board (preferably of the same size) to fit. Lettering on strips makes it much easier to keep letters and margins even; there is little chance of down-hill slope; mistakes can be discarded easily; strips are easy to save and reuse; and the strips are also an excellent design device. If one has several blocks of text (descriptions of services or types of material), they can be placed on blocks of poster board. The blocks will be easy to arrange on the displays and easy to store and re-use at a later time, either together or in different combinations.

Figure 59 illustrates some of the advantages and problems involved in using strips of text. This particular poster is crammed with information, so the layout was kept as simple as possible; margin lines are exact on three sides, all of the strips are the same height, and the cartoon is in line with strips at both top and bottom. The strips were cut to fit the available space, and the text was then edited to fit the strips. Some of the directions are not as clear as they might have been, but the message had to be made to fit the limited space available on the strips. Had lettering errors been made, only one strip would have had to be redone; the uniform size of the strips adds unity to a poster which otherwise might have been confusing; the strips contrast effectively with the dark background; and all of the poster ingredients can be removed and re-used at another time.

Layout

Many of the problems and solutions which have been considered involve not only lettering, but layout as well. Layout, quite simply, is a "laying out" of shapes or design ingredients in a coherent, balanced, and effective manner. And that is what must be done with all design components: cartoons, captions, lettering strips or blocks, arrows, yarn, etc. Posters are usually executed on one piece of board and must be sketched and completely planned before any of the elements are prepared; once the board is completed it is almost impossible to make any changes in arrangement. This is not the case when one is using separate design components. The layout should be planned in advance, but the layout may also be changed at any time.

Here is how layout might work in operation: Suppose one wishes to make a poster on a standard 22- by 28-inch piece of poster board. A cartoon similar to the one in the previously discussed poster is to be used; the caption selected is "Need Some Escape Reading?"; and it is decided to make the board horizontal with the 28-inch length for the width. In order to allow space for margins at the ends of the caption, the caption strip should be about 25 or 26 inches long and about 3½ or 4 inches high, depending on the size of lettering used. The caption should be penciled in lightly so that one can see how it fits; the spacing must be even before the letters are painted and outlined.

After the cartoon and caption have been laced on the board (but not affixed to it), one can determine how much space is left for the text. If, for example, four types of reading matter are to be listed, four strips can be cut to size. Figure 60 shows how the strips might be lettered; the longest word or phrase is done first to establish the lettering size, and then the other words are cen-

DON'T BE CONFUSED!

"B" (BIOGRAPHIES) ARE IN YOUNG TEEN ROOM

"R" (REFERENCE BOOKS) - ASK AT INFORMATION DESK

"Δ" (YT BOOKS) ARE IN THE YOUNG TEEN ROOM

BOOKS WITHOUT NUMBERS ARE FICTION AND ARE SHELVED ALPHABETICALLY BY AUTHOR'S NAME

NON-FICTION BOOKS: 000-799 ARE UPSTAIRS 800-900 ARE ON MAIN FLOOR IN THE BACK

IF STILL CONFUSED, ASK LIBRARIAN FOR HELP

59

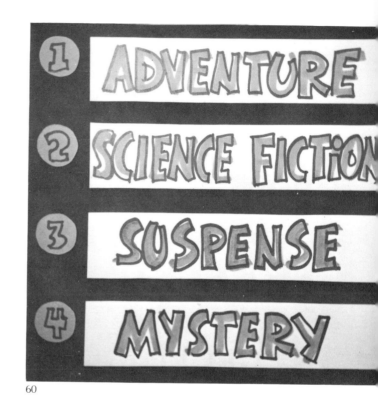

1 ADVENTURE

2 SCIENCE FICTION

3 SUSPENSE

4 MYSTERY

60

tered on the remaining strips. After the strips have been lettered, they can be "tried on" for size and balance.

Check the margins: if possible, the right edge of the lettering strips should line up with the end of the caption strip; the top and/or bottom of the cartoon might be in line with the top or bottom of one of the strips; and, depending on the length of the caption and the size of the cartoon, the left edge of the caption could be lined up with the left edge of the cartoon. Figure 61 shows how the design pieces might be laid out; in this case it has been possible to have even margins on all four sides, but that is not always necessary or possible.

Check the contrast: do the display components stand out against the background or should the contrast be heightened? The strips might contrast with the background more effectively if they were set off in some way. Black rug yarn might help. In Figure 62 the strips have all been moved in to allow space for the yarn, and in Figure 63 a yarn rectangle encloses the strips (and the yarn lines up with the other elements in the design). The yarn pulls the strips together in a tighter design unit, and it also adds contrast. Now let's try something else. Perhaps the strips would show up even better glued to a piece of black poster board as shown in Figure 64 (and note that the black rectangle has been cut the same height as the cartoon and lined up with it and with the caption). This provides even better

contrast. But the poster is still a bit dull; perhaps there are too many rectangles. Numbered orange circles might add dash, and Figure 65 shows how they enliven the poster.

There are other ways in which the same poster components may be used, but first it might be helpful to summarize a few points:

1. The design components should contrast effectively with the background
2. The lettering style for the text should be uniform and the caption may be in a different, but compatible, style
3. The lettering should be penciled in so that the maximum letter size may be determined
4. Margin lines should be considered
5. The caption, cartoon, and text should be attached to poster board with rubber cement and to bulletin board with map tacks
6. All pencil lines should be erased when the poster is completed

Next, let's examine some other possible layouts of the basic components. Figure 66 shows how the board might look with the cartoon replaced by a large arrow. In Figure 67 the text and the black backing have been cut into strips and these have been glued to white poster board; a tall, thin arrow has also been added. In Figures 68, 69, 70, and 71, the elements have been arranged on a vertical board. Figure 69 uses a yarn outline arrow, and Figure 70 has a small triangle added to the center of the arrow. Figure 71 is shown with a raised caption. Elements can be raised in a variety of ways; in this case, a small battery box was used as a lift. Figure 72 shows the box attached to the board. The box was stapled from the inside, but it might have been glued or tacked to the bulletin board; after the box was attached to the board, the caption was affixed to the front of the box. These are only a few of the many ways in which the same ingredients may be used, but they give an indication of the variety which is possible.

Cartooning

Lettering and layout are often easier to do than one might think, but cartooning presents a different problem since it is usually more difficult than it might appear to be. However, most of the cartoons in this book are rather simple, and if one has any artistic skill the cartoons should not be too difficult to copy. For one with no skill whatsoever, copying them could be an impossible task. But, no matter how lacking in talent one might be, there are cartoons which can be executed. Anyone who can trace a circle can draw a cartoon.

The first step in drawing a cartoon is to make a circle with a marking pen; a compass circle may be drawn and traced, but it is usually easier to draw around a suitably sized lid, glass, or bowl with the marker. Figure 73 shows three rows of cartoon faces; all are circles with ears added. The steps in making a basic face are shown in the first strip: add two circles for eyes; add a U

for a nose; add a mouth; add pupils (in this example they are looking down and left, but they can look in any direction); add hair. All of the faces in the second strip are built on the basic face; the only differences are the placement of the pupils, the shape of the mouth, and the hair. Some variations of eyes and noses are shown in the third strip. The basic face can fill most cartooning needs with only three changes: the pupils can be moved to direct attention to another part of the design; the mouth can be smiling or frowning; and the hair can be changed or a hat can be used.

The face is the most important part of any cartoon figure, but the hands can also be very important. There are only two basic uses for cartoon hands—holding and pointing; when there is nothing for them to hold or at which to point, they can be hidden. Figure 74 shows a row of cartoon hands. The three sets of hands are in a holding position; the first set is the easiest to make, but if one wants to be a bit more professional the others can be used. If these hands are cut out, they can be used to hold a sign or object from the top, bottom, or sides. The last hand in the strip is pointing and it may be pointing at almost anything: a sign, lift panel, pamphlet holder, textual material, book jackets.

Now that we have faces and hands, we need a body to which they can be attached. Two kinds of stick figures are shown in Figure 75. The first type has a shoulder and hip line, and the second

61

62

63

64

65

66

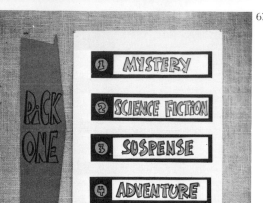

67

68

69

71

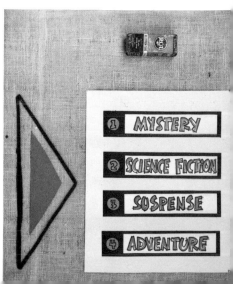

74

75

76

has a rib cage and pelvic area. These figures can be used to show movement of any kind; when movement is to be shown, the most important thing to keep in mind is that the shoulders and hips move in opposite directions: if the left shoulder is down, the left hip is up; and if the right shoulder is down, the right hip is up. Figure 76 shows a different kind of body style, and this style is probably the easiest to make and the most effective. The three basic body positions are shown in Figure 76: standing (with hands hidden), pointing, and holding. Figure 77 shows all of these basic cartoon faces, hands, and bodies doing "their own thing."

8. Provisions for art work

The arrangements for art work in a library involve a number of variables: how the cost of supplies fits into the budget, how time for the work is allotted, who does the work, and who supervises the work. In some situations art work of any kind is regarded as a petty-cash, petty-time, and petty-nuisance type of activity. This kind of thinking produces haphazard arrangements and haphazard results. In some libraries art work is considered to be an important facet of the service which the library renders to the patron; when this is the case, the provisions for its inclusion are definite even though they may be limited in scope. The arrangements differ from library to library but there are certain patterns. Some of these operational patterns will be discussed and then possible improvements will be suggested.

Budget and supplies

The first problem to be considered is the budget. It may be that art work, in your library, is a budget item; in too many libraries it is not. There are many possible reasons for its exclusion from the budget, but, in many cases, the chief reason is that the budget makers simply see no reason

for including it. Many people still regard art work as mere decoration—a few holiday decorations, a few pictures or photographs, or perhaps a bit of student work. The decoration factor is relevant (libraries and schools are discovering that décor has an important psychological effect on patrons and students), but the educational and informational aspects of posters and displays are of greater import. Art work can contribute significantly to the service provided by the library, and, therefore, it should be a budget expense. With the growing recognition of the importance of audio-visuals, art work might be included as "educational visuals." Selling art work as a budget item may not be easy, but it is necessary if we are really to sell our books and services to patrons.

It might be mentioned that some library systems provide a few basic art supplies and consider that adequate. It is not. There is no way in which a central supply system can anticipate and provide all the materials which might be needed. Even with a central supply system (and an art department), there will always be a few miscellaneous items which will have to be purchased. These may be small items (nails, wire, pieces of wood, a skein of rug yarn, a few yards of burlap), but they may be indispensable and they may be needed immediately for a display in preparation. There should be a budgeted fund, however limited, for purchasing these supplies as they are needed. Such a fund is essential for an efficient publicity program.

Pre-planning of art work

The second problem, or group of problems, is how the time for art work is allotted, who does it, and who is responsible for it. In a one-librarian operation, the librarian may have to produce the ideas and then execute them. Since most librarians have received little or no training in art work of any kind, an inordinate amount of time might be spent in achieving less than satisfactory results. Furthermore, the amount of time spent on displays of one kind or another is probably stolen from the time that the librarian feels should be spent on more professional duties. A clerk or student helper may be available to execute the displays, but in all probability the librarian still has the responsibility of planning the display program (there should be an over-all plan regarding the kind of displays to be done and a set schedule for changing displays). The librarian should know enough about art work to make specific suggestions and to evaluate results according to some established criteria. The art work in the library should be a carefully designed, scheduled activity that is carried out with a defi-

nite purpose (other than decoration) in mind.

In a larger library, the individual librarian may or may not be directly involved in the preparation of displays. There may be a talented member of the staff who does most of the art work, or the job may be passed around on a rotating basis—or any form of art work may be almost totally ignored except for an occasional exhibit of library materials. But even if there is no direct involvement in the execution of art work, there should be concern with what is being done (or what is not being done), particularly in regard to the departments of the library. Displays are vital to the kind of service provided and therefore should be a part of the librarians' professional concern. This is as applicable in academic libraries as it is in public and school libraries. Librarians should have ideas and suggestions to contribute, and it should be kept in mind that at some time in the course of a professional career one may be obliged to do or supervise art work.

The librarian and the artist

There are, of course, many large systems which maintain a separate art department. For librarians in a small system, such a department probably sounds like the answer to all problems. While it is helpful, it still does not absolve the librarian from initiative or responsibility. The library may be supplied with signs and posters on a regular basis, but these will do little to fill many of the bulletin board needs (one should not tack up a printed sign or poster and call it a bulletin board display); moreover, most of the materials provided by the art department may be sized to meet reproduction requirements rather than library display requirements. In some systems, when librarians request materials to use for bulletin board displays, there are often delays in filling the request and discrepancies between what is asked for and what is supplied.

Even with access to professional art work on a regular basis, there is the problem of effectively using the standard signs and posters provided; if special materials can be requested, there is the problem of deciding what is needed and in communicating the need in terms which the artist will understand. It must be kept in mind that it is the librarian who knows the library resources and services and the needs of the patrons. The artist may be a professional in his or her field but may know nothing about the library; it is the responsibility of the librarian to determine what the patrons should be told about the library and of the artist to decide *how* to tell it visually.

Some suggestions for change

Following are some suggestions for improving the situation. It has already been mentioned that one of the first steps is to get art work into the budget; that is almost a *sine qua non*. The second step is to plan the art work in advance: decisions must be made as to what the messages will be, what forms they will require, what general supplies will be needed; and then some kind of schedule must be made with definite work time allotted to get the job done. If a definite plan is built around what information should be communicated to the patrons, it will be possible to arrange a timetable which will allow for the making of the more or less permanent displays (floor plans, directional signs, self-help displays) and of temporary displays (bulletin boards, book cart displays, quizzes, and so on). In a larger library it might be arranged for some of the temporary displays to become rotating displays, moving from one section or department of the library to another. No temporary display should be left up for more than six weeks unless it is changed in some way or moved to a new location.

Part of the planning, of course, involves deciding who is going to do the work and when. If the librarian is doing the display, he or she should have most of the materials ready to go up before taking down the old display; if one gets behind schedule, and a display has been up too long, then there should be a few fillers or instant quizzes to be put up while the new display is being prepared. A bulletin board should not be left empty for more than a day or two; an empty board is an indication of poor planning and a source of irritation to many. If clerks or assistants are doing the board, they should be allowed sufficient time to prepare the materials; they should not be expected to fit that task in between their other assignments.

Another suggestion is that the librarian acquire some basic art skills and much of this book is directed toward that end. This applies whether the librarian is supervising or doing the work. If the librarian is supervising the work, he or she should be able to help and direct the person who is doing it, and it should be seen to that the doer is given every assistance in mastering the necessary techniques. The training should not be a sink-or-swim, learn-on-the-job process, and no one should be expected to do it that way—even though that may have been your introduction to art work in the library. An idea file of previous displays should be kept (with photos, if at all possible); and there should be a file of previously used components and of any display ingredients (book jackets, photographs from discarded books, publishers' brochures with sample pages) which might be useful.

A final suggestion is that arrangements be made to hire someone to do the basic art work for the library. However assiduously a librarian may work toward improving his or her art skills, it must still be admitted that some art work done by a professional or an art student would be of tremendous help to the individual librarian and to the program. Getting the necessary funds undoubtedly presents a problem. Funds may not be available on a permanent basis, but it might be possible to obtain funds for a one-time expenditure. The best selling point might be that in the long run it would be more economical to hire a professional to make reusable components than for the librarian or other members of the staff to spend valuable time (stated in cost-per-hour figures) trying to do something which could be done better and more cheaply by someone else.

Assuming that funds are available for this kind of arrangement, a great deal of advance planning must be done. One must anticipate what cartoons, captions, and signs could be best used, and re-used, over a period of time. The materials used must be durable (no construction paper); cartoons should be on poster board with wide margins (so that the edges can be trimmed if they become frayed) and most of them should cover one fourth to one third of the bulletin board space; captions should also be on poster board with wide margins, and some of the captions should be large enough so that a caption and cartoon placed side by side will extend almost the full length of the bulletin board. A few small, multi-purpose easel or stand-up figures should also be commissioned.

If a competent art student can be located, it might be possible to get by with five dollars for each cartoon and caption set and one dollar more for each additional caption. Those would be absolutely minimum rates, probably, and the supplies would have to be furnished by the library. If an advanced art student or a professional is hired, the rates will be higher but the quality should be better. The number of cartoons and captions obtained will, of course, depend on the amount of money available; and it is for the librarian to decide which display materials will be of most use to the library. The materials should be used and stored carefully.

When working with an artist, whether commissioned or employed by the system, the librarian should not be intimidated by the artist's rather specialized skills. Publicity for the library should be a cooperative effort between the librarian, the expert on the library, and the artist who is to convey the librarian's message visually.

The librarian should be as explicit as possible about what is wanted and, if possible, should show examples of the type of work desired. The artist should be offered a choice of content and form. Some things visualize better than others, and if a specific effect or message is to be conveyed, the artist will often have to try several approaches to decide which one is most effective. After the artist understands exactly what it is that is needed, he or she may have suggestions to offer about how it can be done or how the message could be changed somewhat for a better effect. Even though the librarian should start out with something definite in mind and should be the final judge of the results, all suggestions of the artists should be considered. The librarian should not abdicate control but should cooperate, maintaining as the objective the best interests of the patron. The artist, as the expert on materials and techniques, should make decisions on materials, color, and design.

There is another possibility which it might be worth while to consider. It was mentioned in an earlier chapter that a collection of wood or fiberboard geometric shapes would be useful to have on hand: they would be more permanent and less easily damaged than poster-board shapes; they could be painted easily or covered with fabric; display materials can be easily attached to them; and their thickness adds an interesting dimensional element to any display. Some doodling will determine how many large shapes can be cut from 4- by 8-foot sheets of material; allowance must be made for negative shapes—that is, sufficient margin should be left and the shapes cut out "whole." The carpenter may start the cut from the edge of the board and work toward the shape (this cut can be filled in later with plastic wood), or, in some cases, the cut can be started in the center of the board.

It might be possible to get the shapes cut out at a lumber yard for a small fee, and, if not, it will probably be possible to locate someone with a home workshop. Competent woodworkers are usually easier to locate than competent artists, so someone may be found to do the work free; if not, a flat fee can be paid for the job. The cutting should be worked out on graph paper before the board is purchased, and it should be explained carefully to the carpenter that he is to keep the negative, background shapes in one piece. The cut shapes can be waxed or stained (if of wood), painted, or covered with burlap.

9. Idea sources

You have now been exposed to most of the basics of display work—purpose of displays, types of messages, varieties of form, and techniques of designing and executing the different types—but you may still lack ideas for your own artwork. The search for motifs is a constant poser, and this paucity of ideas often leads to a reliance on the tried, true, and trite standard approaches. But it is the non-standard approach which draws interest and sells the message or product; and it is necessary to find a non-standard slant or add an individualizing twist to the standard one. There are a number of productive idea areas, and a survey of the possibilities should be helpful in the search for new solutions.

The product

The first idea area is the product itself. What in particular is being sold? and is it an object, a service, or an idea? After deciding exactly what is being offered to the public, determine what there is about the specific product which will appeal most at the specific time it is being offered. If it is a standard item or service (type of reading material, information source, group activity, program, or exhibit) which is being presented, the feature that makes it unique or of special interest should be emphasized. If it is an idea which is being sold, it must be established why this idea is of special interest, and it then must be presented in such a way as to awaken this interest.

In the library the product involved is usually books and information or information sources. It is possible, of course, to attempt selling all of the books and services at one time with a "Read Books" or "Use the Library" approach. This type of publicity might be appropriate for a national campaign intended to direct attention to the library as a public institution, but it will do little toward promoting the use of a particular library and its resources. Any national or area campaign can be used to help sell the local library and its services, but it is the services and products of a particular library with which this book is concerned. Therefore, an analysis of the product line and its salable features should suggest some publicity techniques.

Books

Books are the most basic of a library's products. For purposes of publicity, it is most effective to deal with those attributes of books which are most easily recognized by the general public or which can most easily be promoted in one way or another. Four of the most salable qualities are newness, topicality, reading interests or aversions, and adaptability to various sales gimmicks. The first three qualities are familiar and acceptable to most librarians, but the fourth, adaptability to gimmicks, may be totally unacceptable to many. There may be some librarians who will flinch at all of the attributes named because of the seemingly total disregard for literary merit. The objection is a valid one; but, unfortunately, undiluted literary merit is of interest to few members of the public; therefore, it is often necessary to emphasize what may be a secondary attribute of a significant book. This does not mean that books should be purchased with only salability in mind, but it does mean that circulation of "good" books can be increased by using promotable qualities and current publicity techniques. The publicizing of good books renders an important service to the public and to the cause of good reading, and it should not be overlooked.

New books have an intrinsic salability due to the mere physical newness, the fresh jacket, and clean, unmarked pages; and a newly published work has other compelling features. People have a special interest in keeping *au courant,* and keeping up with the new books is one way of doing so; additional impetus is supplied by the reviews, by author interviews in the press and on TV, and by word of mouth. Usually the library needs only to put these books in a New Books section to attract the pre-sold market. There is a similar secondary interest in new editions of books either in hardcovers or paperback if attention is directed to their newness and they are not put immediately into the regular collection. If the new editions are not re-reviewed, it might be worth while to post copies of the original reviews or excerpts such as those in *Book Review Digest* or Moulton's *Library of Literary Criticism.*

Older books can often be made to seem new, or at least newer, by association with new books. The term *best seller* has an ever-constant newness, and this can be exploited by a display of last year's best sellers, best sellers of the past five years, or even fifty years of best sellers. Another possibility is a retrospective display of literary award-winning books; reviews of a current winner could be posted near an exhibit of the earlier winners of that award. Still another technique is to have groupings of other books by current best-selling or award-winning authors. Here, too, copies of the original reviews would be informative and would add interest to the display. All of these techniques use new books to promote interest in older books which might still be attractive if readers were reminded of them. Being on the alert for ways in which to remind them is an important service.

The second salable quality mentioned is topicality; this term can apply to seasons, sports, music, TV shows, Broadway plays, films, and current events of international, national, and local interest. Librarians make use of many of these "topicals," especially seasons, holidays, and vacations; but there are others which are ignored and the standard ones could use some new twists. Many standard events lend themselves to a dual type of display: for men and women and/or for likes and dislikes. For example: a display of books relating to the sport of the season and a tandem display of books for golf, baseball, or football widows might be arranged; there might be a display of books "For People Who Like Sports," and another "For People Who Don't Like Sports ... But Like to Know What's Happening" (included might be books on sports personalities of general interest and basic books about sports). In an election year displays could promote books candidates should read and books their wives should read. During the theater, opera, symphony, or ballet season, there could be books for *aficionados* and for neophytes. The same approach could be used for seasons (some people like certain seasons and others don't), for vacation time (for travelers and for stay-at-homes), and for many other items of current interest.

Some of the current events which are often ignored are those relating to aspects of the world of entertainment and the arts. There could be groupings of books which have been made into films, plays, or TV shows. At awards time (Oscar, Emmy, Tony, Grammy) there could be collections of books by and about celebrities and about show business in general. This type of topical exhibit can be particularly effective at the local level. If there are amateur theater, dance, music, or art groups in your area, a library display could be arranged to coincide with some of their activities. The groups or clubs would, in all probability, be delighted to loan the library materials to be used for a coordinated exhibit; a related film program, slide show, lecture, or discussion group might also be initiated. This type of programing can be extremely important in establishing rapport with organizations, and it can also render a significant service to the community.

A third sales approach is to capitalize on the reading interests and antipathies which we all cherish. A grouping of atypical mysteries could be sold with the caption "Mysteries for People Who Don't Like Mysteries." The same approach could be applied to almost any type of reading: westerns, science fiction, historical novels, suspense stories. A similar approach might be used to extend reading tastes; nonfiction books about the West or novels with a western setting might be sold with the caption "If You Like Westerns, You Might Like These." Mystery fans might like certain types of suspense fiction or nonfiction books about crime, criminals, and police work; readers of historical novels could be encouraged to read nonfiction historical books; and readers of Gothic novels might also be directed elsewhere. This type of selling requires a thorough knowledge of books and reading interests and a creative appraisal of ways and directions in which these interests might be extended.

Grouping books according to those which a prominent or historical figure should read or should have read was mentioned previously. Ask members of the staff or patrons for some ideas along these lines. In a school library this kind of approach could work particularly well since students, particularly the younger ones, can present fresh and original ideas. If this is made an assignment or a contest, the student should be asked to select a given number of books (chosen from those in the library) and to tell why these books were selected. The winning lists and the selected books could be the basis for the display, which might perhaps be made permanent, with the personage, lists, and books changed monthly. It might also be possible to ask prominent people in the community, people well known to the public, or members of the staff or faculty to recommend books which they have found particularly enjoyable or informative. The personal recommendation technique is an effective device and also good for public relations since the people whose opinions are sought will probably be flattered.

The fourth category of salable features, adaptability to gimmicks, is really a catch-all to cover miscellaneous publicity techniques. Some of the possible angles are groupings based on time, place, nationality, and occupation. Time groupings could cover works by and about authors of a decade, period, or century; works about artists, playwrights, and musicians of the selected period could also be included. A grouping could be based on books written in, or pertaining to, a certain period and these could be subdivided into fiction and nonfiction. If a two-sided display cart is available, the across-the-cart sign could read "American History" and "In Fact" could be on one side and "In Fiction" on the other. The "In Fact/In Fiction" device can be used with any event or period of time which has been well covered by both historians and novelists.

The place technique could bring together works of writers from various areas ("Writers from the South"), specific cities ("The Parisians," or "American Writers in Paris"), or books about a specific geographical area. Groupings based on nationality will depend on the amount of material available; there may not be enough books for a display on writers from individual foreign countries, but there may be enough for a "Writers from Abroad" exhibit. Some professions have been well covered in both fact and fiction and they too can be used as a theme. It might be well to keep in mind that all these displays can be made more compelling and more informative if non-book materials are used also; maps, photographs, reproductions, manuscripts, and related materials should be included whenever possible.

Use of a "For Men/For Women" caption has already been mentioned, but there are innumerable variations on the grouping which can be used with most of the standard book displays. A display of books "For the House" could include books on maintenance, repair, and woodworking for the men, and decorating, cooking, and child care for the women. Books on hobbies, finance, health, exercise, and business could also be divided in this way. A division based on age can be used, but care must be taken with the terminology. The caption "For the Young/For the Old" is not acceptable but some of the paired captions which might be used are "For Teenagers/For Their Parents"; "For Newlyweds/For In-Laws"; and "For Parents/For Grandparents." These split displays are particularly effective because patrons are intrigued by the division and usually look at the materials in both displays.

Information sources

Suppose, however, that what is being sold is an information source rather than a book. Here, too, the product and the patron must be considered: what is there about a particular source which the patron might find interesting, unusual, or difficult: Play up that feature. Offer some interesting, curious, or unexpected information available in the source; put the information in the form of a quiz. If the source is one which might be intimidating to an uninitiated user,

that fact might be recognized and made light of with a "Don't Be Afraid of An Index" (or bibliography, concordance, thesaurus). When sources are being promoted, the interests and needs of the public must be carefully considered; students and adults require different approaches and need to be sold on different sources.

Services

If what is being sold is a service, the publicity should make it clear why the service is offered, to whom it is available, and how it can be obtained. If it is a service for the general public, that should be made clear, and if it is a service for a segment of the public (the shut-in, blind, foreign, or researcher) that also should be brought out. Some of the operational details of the service might be explained so that the public will be more understanding of any possible snags or delays. It might, for instance, be explained how requests for material from other libraries are handled, and why there is often a delay in getting the material; if any charge is involved, the reason for it should be explained. Unless services are carefully sold and made clear, they can be a source of irritation rather than good will.

The aforementioned "Don't Be Afraid" technique may be used with the reading or copying machines in the library. Many patrons are wary of even the simplest machine and require some introduction to its use. A "Don't Be Afraid" or

"It Doesn't Bite" caption may be used to introduce a few of the basic operating details, and a note to the effect that the librarian will be glad to assist in the use of the machine should be added. Since some patrons seem to feel that materials are microfilmed solely for the convenience of the library, it might be explained that microfilming enables the library to provide more materials than would otherwise be possible. Here too, if there is any charge for using any of the materials or machines the reason for it should be explained.

Ideas

There are occasions when the library will be selling ideas, and the same type of analysis regarding reasons and aims applies. It should be established why a given idea will, or should, appeal to the audience. The message should be as specific as possible. A "Read More" sign is almost totally useless unless the patron is also told why he or she should read more or at all. It might be emphasized that certain books can help people on the job or in business, while others can help with hobbies or other recreational interests and can provide information which might be useful in the areas of finance, family life, health, and travel. If the library is encouraging support of organizations or activities, it should be spelled out why people should be interested and what benefits might accrue to them, their families, or their community through their support of the idea that is being promoted.

Patron interest

All of the sales techniques described above are geared to the product being presented; but a second idea area is concerned with the particular clientele: their interests and the current expressions they use. What are the interests of your patrons? What is happening in your city? What sport or TV shows are in season? What recordings are top sellers? Some of these items have already been covered under the heading of products, but here the chief concern is with caption ideas produced by patron interest. Certain current expressions have almost instant appeal; such expressions may be all-purpose or they may be related to a single activity.

Some of the all-purpose expressions which have been used extensively are "Would You Believe ...?," "Cool It, Baby," "Come Where It's Happening," "Tell It Like It Is," and so forth. These phrases produce an immediate reaction (even if it is distaste for this type of slang), and they make compelling captions. However, they must be up to date; last month's "in" expression may be "out" this month and if dated slang is used the younger patrons will be convinced that the library is definitely not in style. Captions based on the top ten songs or on movies which have attracted special interest are other possibilities; the best way to find out what is happening is to ask a teen-ager.

Sports have wide appeal and expressions relating to them are most effective with young people. Examples of such are "Steal Home: Use a Subject Index," "For a Shoe String Catch on Current Info, Use *Readers' Guide*," "Lateral to a Yearbook for Newer Stuff," "Don't Balk; Ask the Librarian for Help." Timing is important with sports expressions, and care should be taken not to use baseball expressions during the football or basketball season. And here too one must be on the alert for new trends; the popularity of hockey and soccer is spreading, and if your community or school has an interest in these sports, that should be kept in mind.

Slang and sports jargon have their greatest vogue among teen-agers and young adults and are effective in a school library, but many phrases are also helpful in a public library. If there is a separate section for young people, they might be used there; if not, a few might be used anyway. Adults are likely to be familiar with current expressions—even though they may not use any of them—so they are still an attention-getting device. Try some of them out; the experiment will at least dent the edges of the library's often stodgy image.

Idea file

A third productive source of ideas is an idea file. Any interesting, clever, unusual, or well-drawn cartoon or drawing should be clipped from newspapers and magazines (not from current library copies, of course). It is unnecessary to have specific use in mind for the clipping; anything which attracts attention should be clipped and put into a folder. When an idea is needed, just sorting through the folder may be helpful. Cartoon characters could be used with the captions "Did You Hear?," "Is It True (What They Say About the Periodical Room)?," "Is It For Real (that the Library Has 10,000 Volumes)?"; or captions could be used saying, "Don't Be So Upset (Use ... as a Reference Source)," "Don't Just Stand (or Sit) There, Use a ...." There are numerous possibilities, and one cartoon can suggest any number of ideas and captions.

If a similar cartoon can be executed, or if someone can be located to do it, most of the problem is solved. No copyrighted cartoon or cartoon character may be reproduced without permission of the artist, but it is usually acceptable to use similar cartoons for bulletin boards or for posters which will not be reproduced. If your cartoon is copied from a comic strip or from the work of a cartoonist with a highly individual style, it is best to make some acknowledgment of the source. If, for example, you use a character from *Peanuts* on a bulletin board, you might add a note at the bottom: "With apologies to Charles Schulz."

If no one is available to draw a similar cartoon, the caption suggested by the cartoon clipping might be sufficient by itself. The clipping file should be constantly added to, and nothing should be discarded once it has been used; many of the same ideas may be used over and over again with only a slight variation or sometimes none at all. It may be that the system has an art department or that the library is able to hire the services of an artist for a limited time. In this case, cartoons from the file can be of great assistance in helping to decide exactly what is needed in the way of art work, and in explaining the needs to the artist.

Junk box

A fourth source of ideas is a junk box; the size and type of the junk saved will depend on the available space and one's pack-rat talent. The junk collected might include pieces of fabric and wood, old keys, used batteries and flash bulbs, cord, broken eyeglasses, travel brochures, thread spools, damaged phonograph records, discarded pieces of clothing, fragments from broken toys — just about anything which might possibly be used for future display. One need have no particular use in mind; that will come later.

Some of the things you might do with the junk:

Cover half a bulletin board with old flashlight batteries and use the caption "Power Up With ..." (type of book).

Cover a large area with playing cards and use "It's in the Cards ... That This Will Interest You" or "Tell Your Own Future" (with a display of vocational books).

Use rows of paper plates with "Fill Them Up With Good Food Ideas" (and display a collection of cook books).

Use light bulbs with "Brighten Up Your Reading Interest" (or knowledge in some special area).

Glue play money to poster board to sell books on finance, consumer education, or business. Displays of this kind are limited only by the imagination (which can be stretched with use), and little art work is required other than the caption.

These miscellaneous scrap items may also be combined with cartoon figures or poster-board cutouts. Cartoon figures can be wearing hats, gloves, sunglasses, neckties, handkerchiefs, buttons or bows, dime-store jewelry, and items of clothing. A figure, for example, might have a fist full of play money or hold a card hand, a travel brochure, a paper plate, a shopping bag, a sign, a book, or a book jacket; it might be leaning against a sign, a real board fence, or a wall (stone- or brick-textured paper or vinyl) or sitting on a box, a fence, a book, a tightrope, a board teeter-totter, or a stepladder made of scrap wood. A cutout of a house could have a balsa wood door or shutters, a brick or stone front, fabric curtains; a bus or car cutout could have tires from an old toy, plastic windows, and fabric luggage tied on top. The cartoons, cutouts, and the junk should be saved for reuse either separately or together.

Borrowing

A fifth idea area is the borrowing (adapting or liberating) of any idea or object which might be of use in library displays. There is no copyright on ideas, so anything can be adapted from professional magazines, the suggestions of other librarians and teachers, advertisements. Particularly good sources from which to borrow are department store displays; window decorators are especially ingenious at creating displays from simple materials and common objects, and studying their methods should be helpful (and the library just might be able to borrow some display materials from the stores). A specific exhibit idea might suggest a useful item, but often an object will suggest the idea for the display. A wheelbarrow can be used to show books on gardening; an old suitcase or trunk might be used for travel books; books on outdoor cooking could be placed in a barbecue grill; a small buffet could be used for books on entertaining. Some light objects could be used as part of a bulletin-board arrangement: children's lawn rakes or snow shovels, an umbrella or beach umbrella, a beach towel (with a cartoon figure stretched out on it), a jack-in-the-box. The objects are usually easy to acquire; it is the ideas which are often difficult to find. Seeing objects and ideas in terms of their possible usefulness in displays is a bent which can be cultivated; however, during the growth process, borrow freely.

10. Technical details and miscellaneous display ideas

Unquestionably, technical information of any kind is, by its very nature, dull. Some people have a mechanical aptitude which enables them to grasp "how to" instructions immediately; therefore they may be bored by instructions which are, for them, unnecessary. Others have a mental block which makes even the most simple assembly details seem complicated and formidable. The illustrations and discussion to follow attempt to accommodate both groups. The quick-study people will probably derive sufficient information from the illustrations, and the rest may have to plod along, referring from illustrations to instructions and back to illustrations. Try to keep in mind that all construction methods are simple even though the directions may not seem simple; with the exception of bulletin board construction, the basic materials are construction paper, poster board, scissors, map tacks, a stapler, glue, and tape—no hammer, saw, nails, or screws.

Bulletin boards

We will take the exception first; most bulletin board construction does require hammer, saw, nails, and screws. It also requires bulletin board material, which is usually a fiberboard of some type: plywood is too hard a surface to be used easily with tacks or staples. Most fiberboards come in 4- by 8-foot sheets and most lumber yards will cut the sheets into whatever size is desired. The boards may be given a coat of non-glossy paint or covered with a rough-textured fabric such as burlap. Since fabric need only be wrapped around and stapled to the back of the board, this is often the easier method; it also provides an attractive, textured display surface, and the fabric covers and protects the edges of the fiberboard.

If the board is to be used on an easel, nothing more than painting or covering is needed. If the board is to be hung, however, it must be given a backing; and, in order to hide nailheads, it is usually better to take this step before painting or covering the fiberboard. Fiberboard may be screwed or nailed directly to a wall, but that often damages the wall; and, since permanent attachment makes it difficult to change the color or covering of the board, direct attachment is not the preferred method of hanging a board. Fiberboard used alone, moreover, is too soft to hold nails or screws, so another material should be used with it. One method of doing this is to attach a strip of wood (usually a 1- by 2-inch strip of soft pine) to the back of the fiberboard. The strip should be a bit shorter than the width of the board and should be attached to the board near the top. Large-head nails (not small-head finishing nails) are driven through the front of the fiberboard into the wood strip; if the nails are long they can be pounded over from the back. One should then fasten two screw eyes (screws with heads in the form of loops) into the top of the strip, one at each end. A detail is shown in Figure 78; the attaching nail, in the photograph, has been pounded over and the screw eye has been partially screwed in—for actual use it should be screwed in almost to the "eye." The board is now ready to be painted or covered and hung.

A place to hang the board is now needed. If screw hooks (screws with a hooked end) can be attached to the wall, or attached to a strip of wood which has been nailed or screwed to the wall, the screw eyes can be hung on the hooks. If the wall surface will not support the weight of the bulletin board, it might be possible to thread picture wire through the screw eyes and suspend the board from the ceiling molding. The chief advantage of having the board attached with screw eyes and hooks, instead of having it nailed or screwed directly to the wall, is that the board can be easily taken down. It is much easier to prepare a display if the board can be laid out flat while materials are being attached, and a removable board may also be used elsewhere in the library as part of a special display or program. Furthermore, if there are several boards of the same size, and if the sets of screw eyes and hooks are attached the same distance apart, the boards and displays can be switched. A simple change in placement often increases the mileage one can get from a display, and being able to switch boards from one place to another will increase the flexibility of almost any display program.

Pamphlet holders

Libraries often distribute book lists, book marks, public service pamphlets, or pamphlets concerning library services. For want of any other place to display them, they are often simply fanned out on a table or counter where they usually get scattered and receive little attention. Pamphlet holders are a much better solution: the holders keep the materials together in an orderly manner, having the lists or pamphlets "up" rather than "down" assures them of more attention, and pamphlet holders can be a versatile and attractive display ingredient. Holders are easy to make, use, and store.

Figure 79 shows both the cutting of this kind of holder and the method of assembling it. The holders shown were cut from 9- by 10-inch pieces of construction paper, but any size holder can be made, depending on the size of the materials to be displayed. The front and back of the holder are the same size; and the sides, bottom, and two attaching pieces are all the same size.

78

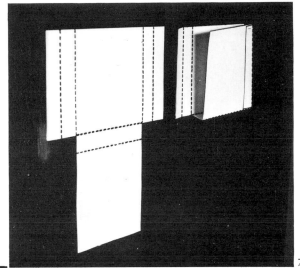

79

80

81

82

The paper is folded on the dotted lines; the back is folded up, the sides are folded around, and the attaching pieces are glued and/or stapled to the back. Figure 80 shows a detail of the assembly; the attaching piece on the right has been glued to the back piece at the bottom (it is difficult to staple the bottom) and it has been stapled at the top. The left side, which is still open in the illustration, is fastened in the same manner.

Figure 81 shows two pamphlet holders in action; the holders were cut from bright-colored construction paper and a geometric design was added with a black marker. For added contrast, the holders were stapled to a piece of black poster board which was then map-tacked to the bulletin board. In this case the board is completed with a simple pointing cartoon and a short caption. The piece of poster board might also be given a prop back and used on a desk or counter top, or it could be "held" by a cartoon figure. Figure 82 shows how the holders may be flattened for storage; the sides and bottom were folded out slightly and pushed flat.

Prop backs

A prop back is a simple device for making a small display board stand up on table tops, counters, and bookcases. It may be used to support small pieces of fiberboard or larger pieces of poster board. Figure 83 shows how a simple prop back may be cut, folded, and attached;

the poster board used for the prop may be cut any size, depending on the size and weight of the board which it will be supporting. The prop is folded along the dotted line and glued so that the bottom of the prop is flush with the bottom of the display board. The triangular flap is folded back to support the display board; the bottom of the flap has to be cut at a slight angle from the horizontal in order for the board to lean back 10 or 15 degrees. Larger or heavier displays may require more of a "lean" for added stability. Metal book ends may also be used for upright props; one simply tapes the back of the display to the back of the bookend.

Shelves

Figure 84 shows the cutting and folding pattern and the bottom view of a simple type of shelf. Poster board is folded on the dotted line (and poster board folds more easily if it is lightly scored or cut along the fold line); the supporting section is stapled or tacked to the bulletin board; a length of yarn or cord is threaded through punched holes at the outer edge of the shelf; and the ends of the yarn or cord are tacked to the board. Figure 85 shows an upper view of the shelf in use. As can be seen in the photograph, the shelf may sag somewhat under weight. It may, however, be used for the display of light paperbacks, for book jackets stiffened with cardboard, or for book jackets placed around styrofoam book dummies.

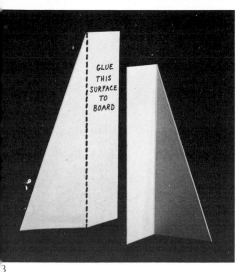

GLUE THIS SURFACE TO BOARD

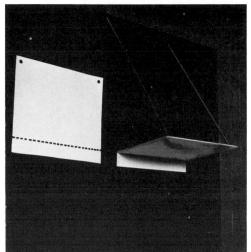

84

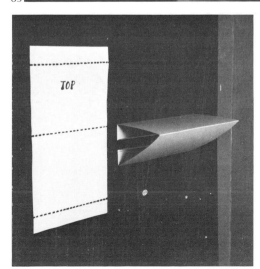

85

86

87

Another, sturdier, type of shelf is shown in Figure 86. In order for the shelf top to be at a right angle to the bulletin board, the bottom support must be at least a few inches longer than the top. The attaching sections are folded along the dotted lines and affixed to the bulletin board. A close-up view is shown in Figure 87. The bottom support makes this type of shelf stronger than the yarn- or cord-supported shelf and more weight can be placed on it.

Three-dimensional devices

Various methods of making design elements three-dimensional have already been discussed, but some details should probably be supplied. Figures 88 and 89 show two different methods. In Figure 88 a three-dimensional caption has been made from one piece of poster board. The board is folded along the dotted lines and the folded ends are attached to the bulletin board with a stapler. In Figure 89 a slightly different method has been used. A separate piece of poster board has been folded into a small box, and the overlapping ends have been stapled together. In the second illustration in Figure 89 the box has been stapled to the bulletin board and small rolls of masking tape have been stuck to the surface; the next step is to stick the caption to the tape. The caption could also be glued to the supporting box. The second method may be used to make almost any design element project; the box can be made of any size and, if a large piece

is to be attached, several boxes of the same thickness can be used. A real box of the right size (a matchbox or cigarette box, for example) may also be used.

Directional arrows

A very useful sign device is shown in Figure 90. A large negative arrow is cut from a bright-colored piece of construction paper or poster board so that a sign can be placed behind it. The first illustration (top left) indicates how the arrow can be cut; the illustration below it shows how the sign can be lettered; and the two illustrations on the right show negative arrows and signs used together. The arrow can be cut to fit into an acetate book cover and the sign can be slipped into the cover behind it. The sign may be placed on top of a cabinet or bookcase to point out materials below, or it can be placed on a bookcase shelf and pointed toward materials above or on either side (the lettering and a prop back would be placed accordingly).

Use of copying machines

Many libraries and school systems have photocopying machines and these can be used for library displays. The maximum size for many machines is 8½ by 13 inches, which is rather small for many display purposes. Figure 91 shows a cartoon figure that has been squeezed into photocopy size; the first illustration shows the original marker drawing, the second shows a negative

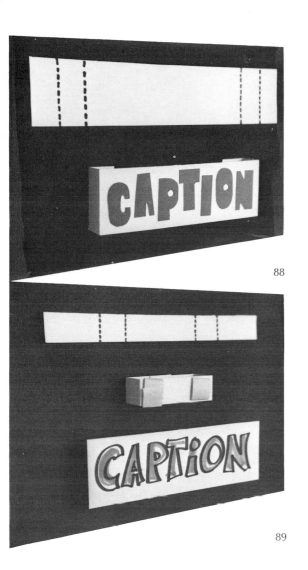

88

89

90

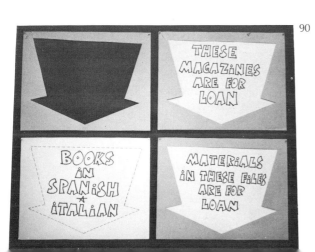

91

92

93

copy, and the third shows the result obtained by running the negative back through the machine. The second step is necessary only with a negative reproduction machine; if the machine produces positive copies, the original can be used to run off as many copies as are desired. If the lines get blurred, as they often do in some machines, they can be touched up with a marking pen.

Figure 92 shows the cartoon pieces cut out and "stretched out" to make an 18-inch-high cartoon; the hands have been hinged from underneath with masking tape. In Figure 93 the cartoon has been given a peaked cap and a book to read. A number of identical figures could be reproduced and used throughout the library, appearing to read books, pamphlets, or magazines. The cartoon has been copied without a mouth so that a smile or frown can be added as the reading material indicates.

Book cart signs

A type of across-the-cart book display is shown in Figure 94. Such a display is meant to be used with a divided book truck which holds books on both sides of a centerpiece. The sign is attached at a right angle to the centerpiece and can then direct attention to both sides of the display. It is particularly effective with the kind of split displays mentioned in the discussion of idea sources (chapter 9). Two other examples of this type of sign are shown in Figure 95, each

with a T shape cut in the center of the poster board. The design at the top is similar to that in Figure 94. In the lower illustration, the crossbar of the T is the same width as the centerpiece of the book truck. The flaps of the T are folded back, and, when the sign is put in place, taped to the centerpiece.

Directional aids

Black numbers on bright yellow poster board were used to make the directional signs shown in Figure 96. The top view indicates the fold lines and the bottom view shows how the sign can be projected in use. The sign is folded in the middle (where black tape has been added for contrast), and the supporting panels are folded back and fastened with rolled or double-faced masking tape. Attached to the ends of bookcases, this kind of sign will enable a patron to look down a row of stacks and go directly to the desired section. Since the numbers are easily seen from a distance, such signs are particularly useful in libraries with balconies.

Quiz board

A quiz board is shown in Figure 97. The board was made by placing six squares with circle cutouts on a larger piece of poster board; the background squares were lettered and the negative circles were numbered. This arrangement could be used for almost any type of matching quiz: authors and dates, characters and novels, poets

94

96

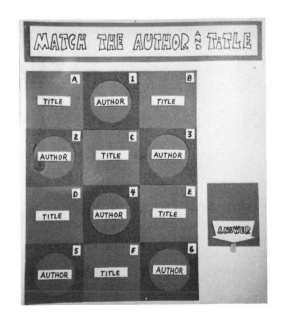

and poems, artists and paintings, cities and states, subjects and Dewey numbers. Answers are listed under a lift panel. The panel is an attractive design element; it is an easy way to post the answers; and the fact that the viewer has to lift the panel adds an intriguing participation factor to the poster.

Lift panels

The panel shown is hinged with tape underneath; Figure 98 shows the view from below with the strip of masking tape for a hinge at the top. Panels may also be hinged by placing tape on the outside at the top. Figure 99 shows the two types placed side by side; the outside tape would be more attractive if it were plastic or cloth tape of a matching or contrasting color. The lift tab is also made with a strip of tape attached at the front and back of the flap, and it has been wrapped around a small piece of poster board to make it more durable. Lift panels may be made in any size or color and they can serve a variety of purposes. They can give answers to quizzes, be used to introduce new services, call attention to special events, or offer miscellaneous information.

Many of the most useful construction methods have been outlined. There are many others which were not discussed and which, possibly, might be even more useful in display work; but only those techniques which involve simple materials and equipment have been presented.

Other books on displays go into greater detail on construction advice; therefore, if such information is needed, it is readily available.

Analysis of displays

Various kinds of displays and layouts have already been discussed, but an analysis of several actual displays—how and why they were executed—might clarify some of the problems and solutions involved in display work.

A strip directory is shown in Figure 100. The display space was limited so only a few of the most requested subjects were included. The directory was of use not only to patrons but also to newer librarians and trainees, who tended to forget many of the specific numbers. The poster board background was red-orange (to coordinate with another red-orange poster in the same area), the division strips yellow, and subject strips white. The division headings were lined up along the right margin to balance that side better; had they been lined up on the left as all the other strips were, the right-hand margin would have been completely erratic. In this case, three copies of all the strips were reproduced on a photocopy machine; these were then cut out and glued to pieces of poster board— and four libraries in the area had the same kind of directory. In one library the board was taped to a bookend and placed on top of the card catalog; in another library the directory was used as part of a bulletin board display; and the other

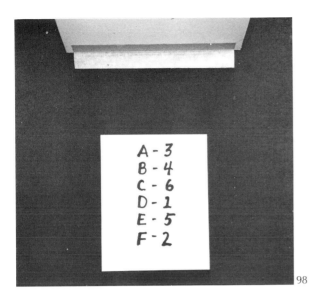

A - 3
B - 4
C - 6
D - 1
E - 5
F - 2

98

ANSWER   LOOK HERE FOR EXCITING NEWS

LIFT   LIFT

99

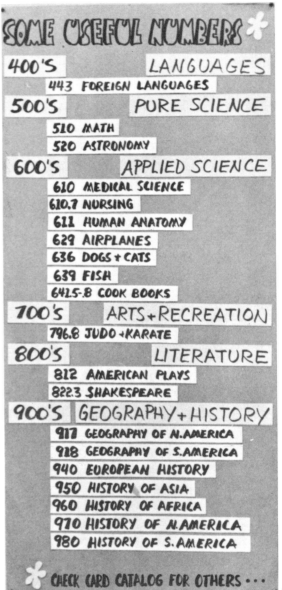

SOME USEFUL NUMBERS ✱

400'S LANGUAGES
443 FOREIGN LANGUAGES

500'S PURE SCIENCE
510 MATH
520 ASTRONOMY

600'S APPLIED SCIENCE
610 MEDICAL SCIENCE
610.7 NURSING
611 HUMAN ANATOMY
629 AIRPLANES
636 DOGS + CATS
639 FISH
6415-.8 COOK BOOKS

700'S ARTS + RECREATION
796.8 JUDO + KARATE

800'S LITERATURE
812 AMERICAN PLAYS
822.3 SHAKESPEARE

900'S GEOGRAPHY + HISTORY
917 GEOGRAPHY OF N. AMERICA
918 GEOGRAPHY OF S. AMERICA
940 EUROPEAN HISTORY
950 HISTORY OF ASIA
960 HISTORY OF AFRICA
970 HISTORY OF N. AMERICA
980 HISTORY OF S. AMERICA

✱ CHECK CARD CATALOG FOR OTHERS ...

100

two libraries taped the display to the ends of bookcases.

The board in Figure 101 was intended to direct attention to the useful but little-used pamphlet file. This is a poster type of bulletin board display; it is larger than the usual poster and it includes heavier materials than could be used with a poster, but it incorporates the elements of poster design—an eye-catching cartoon or shape, a brief caption, and a brief text which can be grasped in a glance. The basic information is conveyed by the caption and pamphlets, but additional information (the list of pamphlet headings) is also available to anyone who might be interested. A metal book display rack was nailed to the bulletin board and string was added to keep the pamphlets from falling out. The list of subject headings was photocopied and the copy sheets fastened in an overlapping lift arrangement.

In Figure 102 the lower cross marks the spot where the patron would be standing while viewing the floor plan; the plan was hung on a bulletin board directly behind the circulation desk. The main purpose of the floor plan was to indicate to the patrons where they were to apply for library cards and also to direct them to the information desk in the next room. The bulletin board used was small—less than two feet in length—so minimum information had to be conveyed with maximum clarity. The plan was executed on red-orange poster board, the broken lines and crosses were yellow, the signs were white, and the areas indicated were shown in black.

Another type of area floor plan is shown in Figure 103. The area was small but it was confusing because the fiction, nonfiction, and biography sections were all run together with no dividing spaces. The background of the floor plan was black poster board and the caption and bookcase shapes were yellow. The number and letter range was color-coded: fiction was shown in red, nonfiction in blue, and biography in green. The young teen area was rather dismal and without bulletin boards, so the floor plan was deliberately rather garish in color and high in contrast. Rolled pieces of masking tape were used to attach the plan to the end of the longer bookcase section.

All of the displays pictured in Figures 100-103 were designed for use in a large and very drab library with poorly placed bulletin board space. The library is located in a disadvantaged area and many of the patrons lack basic information about library organization and materials. For these reasons some of the "rules" for good display have been bent or broken: more colors were used to brighten the surroundings and to direct attention to inconspicuously placed boards, and each display presents more information than is usually advisable. These are only a few of the ways in which display components can be personalized to fit display require-

101

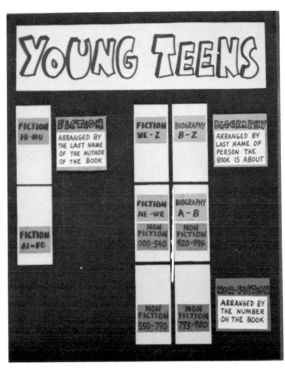

103

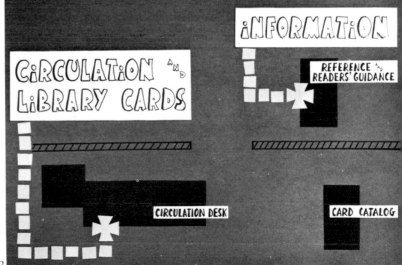

102

ments of an individual library; the size of the library, the size and placement of display space, and the specific clientele are all factors which should be considered.

A final word

In a normal library situation one must also consider the skill and nonskill factors involved in the planning and preparation of displays. Anyone executing or supervising art work should constantly strive to improve on old skills and to acquire new ones—but the nonskill areas must also be acknowledged. Do not attempt more than you can handle. When in doubt stick with the basics—large simple shapes; black and white with one or two bright colors; round-head cartoons; large, simple captions; and, perhaps most important of all, fresh ideas. Display work is not easy, but it is necessary and it can be rewarding. Good luck!

Index